Leading and Supporting Early Years Teams

A practical guide

Deborah Price and Cathy Ota

Routledge
Taylor & Francis Group

LONDON AND NEW YORK

First published 2014
by Routledge
2 Park Square, Milton Park, Abingdon, Oxon OX14 4RN

and by Routledge
711 Third Avenue, New York, NY 10017

Routledge is an imprint of the Taylor & Francis Group, an informa business

British Library Cataloguing in Publication Data
A catalogue record for this book is available from the British Library

Library of Congress Cataloging in Publication Data
Price, Deborah.
Leading and supporting early years teams:
a practical guide/Deborah Price, Cathy Ota. – First edition.
    pages cm
    1. Child development–Great Britain.
    2. Early childhood education–Great Britain.
    3. Early childhood educators–Professional
    relationships–Great Britain. I. Ota, Cathy. II. Title.
    LB1115P93 2014
    372.210941–dc23   2013042615

ISBN: 978–0–415–83919–8 (hbk)
ISBN: 978–0–415–83920–4 (pbk)
ISBN: 978–1–315–77819–8 (ebk)

Typeset in Celeste and Optima
by Florence Production Ltd, Stoodleigh, Devon

Leading and Supporting Early Years Teams

How a staff team works together and how effective and cohesive they are impacts significantly on the children that they care for as well as having implications for the general early years practice and the success of the business of the setting. Drawing together theory and practice this book provides comprehensive guidance on recruiting, supervising and leading an early years team in line with the most recent national guidance.

Focusing on all aspects of leading and supporting a team, the book aims to inspire managers and increase their confidence. It looks at the day-to-day demands of running a setting and the reflective thinking that is needed to establish a vision for a team. The authors consider the skills needed to lead and support a team and offer practical guidance on:

- recruitment, induction, ongoing staff training and supervision;
- disciplinary processes including handling difficult conversations and refocusing a team after a critical incident;
- staff relationships with parents and other professionals;
- involving the team in problem solving and implementing change;
- engaging with the community;
- how to get support for yourself as a manager.

This book will be invaluable support for both new and experienced managers wanting to establish a cohesive and dynamic staff team and provide outstanding childcare provision.

Deborah Price is a Senior Lecturer at the University of Brighton and the Open University, UK.

Cathy Ota is an Independent Education Specialist and Dynamic Consultant and author. She is co-founder of Working With Others, a personalised support and training programme that has been implemented in over 1500 schools and early years settings and is having a dramatic impact on learning and pupil behaviour.

Contents

Contents

Acknowledgements

Deborah Price

With many thanks to students and my colleagues at The Open University and The School of Education at The University of Brighton. My appreciation to the Foundation Degree team and especially Denise Kingston who helped me with material and advice on leadership. My personal thanks as well to the skilled and knowledgeable practitioners in early years that I have worked with, especially Sue Charalambous from See Saw Pre school in Brighton and Hove.

Cathy Ota

Many early years teams and managers have helped contribute to the ideas and insights in this book. My own personal thanks and gratitude goes to the early years settings and managers I have worked with across the UK. I have also had the honour and privilege to work internationally outside of the UK with early years teams. My acknowledgement and appreciation goes especially to Mary Pat Vollick and the team at Mount Hamilton Baptist Daycare – Pumpkin Patch, Ontario, Canada, for all they have taught me in our ongoing partnership and journey together.

CHAPTER 1

Introduction

This book is a product of our combined experience in working with people who work with children – both in early years and through to primary and secondary years. Together we have worked with groups of early years workers, especially early years professionals who have attended a long-term project with us on helping children to work together. Individually, Cathy Ota is an Independent Education Specialist and Team Dynamic Consultant, and one of the co-founders of Working With Others, a programme that teaches children across early years, primary and secondary level how to collaborate, work and learn together as part of a group (see www.workingwithothers.org). Deborah Price, as part of her university role, teaches post-graduate students across the children and young peoples workforce who are interested in developing themselves as leaders and managers. It is out of our individual and combined work that the idea and material for this book came about.

As we have been doing this work individually and together, we have specialized in helping children and adults work with others and one strand of this has been working with early years practitioners in order to improve social skills between children. As we have been talking to students we have realized that in order to be positive role models to children there needs to be high level modelling and understanding of such skills within the staff team. The managers that we have worked with have often expressed their

Introduction

frustration at not being able to inspire their staff team to work together or to manage change in a positive way. Talking and spending time with managers and leaders of early years settings has made us realize that there is a lack of training and guidance in managing and leading staff teams – as though managers are somehow expected to be able to do this as an innate natural skill.

We believe such skills can be studied, learnt and practiced and that most of the difficulties that happen in early years settings are due to a breakdown in inter-adult relationships. We hope that this book gives managers both an insight into an analysis of their role and some reflective points to consider as part of their personal development. It is both a handbook to use to determine practice and a troubleshooting guide for when relations break down.

Managing and leading teams has come under the spotlight recently in light of high profile cases such as the child abuse at a nursery in Plymouth, and the subsequent serious case review that fed into the Tickell review and the reframing of the EYFS. We intend this book to address and provide support for this new guidance and the enhanced expectations of the supervisory role required of early years managers. This role now needs to include regular monitoring and supervision of staff as part of the regulatory requirements. We look at what is necessary to be considered an outstanding setting by OFSTED in regards to leading and managing staff and how managers can take steps on the road to reach and maintain this high level of practice.

For the purposes of this book this is what we mean when we say the manager – we are referring to the person who heads up a setting and combines the role of manager/leader/SENCO. When we refer to early years settings this encompasses pre-schools, crèches and nurseries that are run by committee, privately owned or part of a school. We are also including larger childminder practices where childminders work with each other and sometimes employ assistants.

Change in the workforce

The last twenty years has seen a move towards greater profession-alism and improved training in a workforce that is mainly made up of women in part time, low-paid work. While this is to be welcomed, the now increased expectations of performance at work have not been matched by improved rates of pay and status.

Much of the vocational training focuses on the needs of the child and providing the best possible care and development opportunities for children. This is of course completely necessary and justified. As people involved in the training of the workforce, we have long felt that leaders and managers need the level of training and support when working with their team that is provided in other areas of industry.

In the childcare workforce there seems to be an expectation that these skills are somehow naturally acquired as part of the job or the training that has already been completed. We wonder if this is part of the image of the sector as mainly female and imbued with a caring ethos that permeates to the role of managing and leading and so needs no further enabling.

We are hoping that this book will help to enable childcare workers to be part of the changing workforce in a positive and active way by supporting managers to understand their role as leaders and find ways to support their staff team and also themselves. We also look at the wider community and how the manager needs to place the setting in that community and make positive links with those professionals, parents and carers who come into the setting and those who are part of the community in the vicinity. Siraj-Blatchford and Manni (2007: 22) comment that, 'effective leaders play a key role in the process of establishing a community of learners and team culture among staff. The task is not an easy one'. They go on to quote DuFour in saying that the leader/manager of a setting should have an unrelenting commitment to promote a collaborative environment – even in the face of resistance. We hope that this book will help managers and leaders to do this.

Introduction

Our book has a UK perspective but we think that lessons can be learnt from it that can support and affect practice in early years settings internationally. This is also noteworthy as the present Government has been looking to mainland Europe, especially France, when writing the recent report, 'More Great Childcare', which sets out some key changes in early years childcare in the UK and also indicates the underpinning thinking that seems likely to be guiding policy in the next years to come. These changes are likely to be around staff/child ratios, childminder registration and also the change from a 'satisfactory' rating after inspection to be changed to 'needing improvement'.

The book begins by looking at this report and other contextual policy and legislation in Chapter 2. The chapter gathers in one place the range of guidance and inspection material that relates especially to leadership and management in the legislative structures. However, it also needs to be noted that in order to carry out any of the EYFS and provide a safe and stimulating environment for children there needs to be strong, effective and inspiring leadership in place to move a team towards the settings vision.

Chapter 3 starts this process by examining the stepping-stones of creating a strong and unified team. The chapter breaks down the process of recruitment and provides some reflective points and suggested structures for managers to take note of and incorporate into their own procedures.

Chapter 4 explores the importance of leadership and different leadership styles for early years settings. It considers the elements of what makes a good leader for an early years setting and identifies the ways a leader can develop their organization by reflecting on themselves, their vision and how this is communicated and shared with their team.

Chapter 5 sits alongside Chapter 4's discussion around leadership by turning to examine the features of managing early years teams. The roles of leading and managing are invariably located within the one person in an early years setting. Both roles need to be carefully balanced and are essential when leading an early years setting and team. In acknowledging and appreciating the difference and importance of each we present leading and managing as distinct and separate strands, with their own chapters.

Chapter 6 is about troubleshooting, as the title suggests. It looks at the underpinning difficulties that are connected with early years settings and staff teams and how these contradictions can be managed. It also gives a practical three-point plan for assertion techniques and provides a case study as an example of how conflict can be managed using these steps. The chapter makes some suggestions regarding bringing a staff team together with a united purpose that drives the setting forward.

Chapter 7 looks out to the wider community and how this should be a part of an early years setting. It offers managers suggestions for how they can support their setting, team and children, as well as themselves, by better understanding and drawing on the wider community around them.

Chapter 8 encourages managers to reconsider their responsibility to themselves and how they support themselves professionally and personally so that they can be effective as leaders and managers of their setting.

The conclusion to this book summarises the guidance and material discussed throughout the book. It distills it to a ten-point plan for managers to consider when auditing the staff team, adding to the staff team and reflecting on their own skills and areas for improvement. This section of the book also looks forward in the area of leadership and management to think about the wider arena and how general trends of changing roles of leadership and management are affecting the early years workforce.

References

'More Great Childcare' (2013) www.gov.uk, accessed 9 June 2013.

Siraj-Blatchford, I. and Manni, L. (2007) *Effective Leadership in the Early Years Sector: the ELEYS Study*. London: Institute of Education, University of London.

CHAPTER 2

The background to current professional practice and policy

In this chapter we will be considering the legislative background to leadership and management in the early years. We hope to outline some of the recent changes that have happened in this area of early years practice and move on to look at the implications of these changes. With this chapter in front of them the practitioner should be able to steer a path between what are the requirements in terms of the EYFS, what the OFSTED inspector seeks when carrying out an inspection and finally what is expected from a good and outstanding setting when thinking of leadership and management of staff provision. Using this chapter the manager will have a clear understanding of the key changes in this area and be able to carry out an audit of current provision, matching it with the highest levels of practice and devising an action plan to achieve those standards using the practical next steps section at the end of the chapter.

Professionalism in the early years workforce

This greater emphasis on the management of early years settings is part of a wider trend and slow move towards greater profession-alism in the early years workforce. It is a move that started with the 1989 Children Act and has seen qualification to level three, in addition to suitable experience, as a requirement for managers of settings:

Current professional practice and policy

> We want the people providing care and support to babies and young children to be well qualified and well respected – and for parents to be reassured that their children are receiving the high quality care. We need to move away from the idea that teaching young children is somehow less important or inferior to teaching school-age children.
>
> (www.education.gov.uk, accessed 18 April 2013)

In addition, at present (and currently under review) there must be a minimum of 50 per cent staff trained to level two or above and more recently there has been the introduction of a foundation degree in early years and the Early Years Teaching Status (EYTS). This is a post-graduate qualification comparable to qualified teacher status. This latter qualification has been recently changed from Early Years Professional Status (EYPS) in the latest Government initiative 'More Great Childcare' (January 2013) because

> there is nothing more important in early education than the quality of the staff that are delivering it. As Professor Nutbrown pointed out in her review of qualifications for the early education and childcare workforce, the quality of the workforce and the qualifications on offer at the moment are not good enough. Staff are on low pay and in too many cases lack basic skills.
>
> (More Great Childcare 2013: 6)

Practitioners completing these post-degree qualifications will be expected not only to have achieved a grade C or above (or comparable) in Maths and English as before, but also demonstrate the same level of attainment in Science. This is the same level of pre-course requirement expected of teachers. The difference is that the new EYTS graduates will not be able to achieve actual Qualified Teacher Status (QTS) – even though this was suggested by Professor Cathy Nutbrown (More Great Childcare 2013).

There is an argument that this new enhanced qualification without QTS will not bring higher status and pay to early years workers, but will be part of an argument to higher staff–child ratios, as already proposed in the EYFS review. It is anticipated that the rationale will be that, as staff working in the settings will be better qualified, they will be more able to manage larger groups of children. This proposal has very recently been abandoned but is something that may be mooted again in the future.

In terms of the management and leadership focus of this book, the new standards for EYTS all require best practice in management and leadership in order to be able to achieve them. The EYT (early years teacher) does not have to be the manager of a setting, but if they are not, then they need to be managed and deployed by a leader of great professional ability. The expectations around the role of the EYT include, to:

- Set high expectations which inspire, motivate and challenge all children
- Promote good progress and outcomes by children
- Demonstrate good knowledge of early learning and EYFS
- Plan education and care, taking into account the needs of all children
- Adapt education and care to respond to the strengths and needs of all children
- Make accurate and productive use of assessment
- Safeguard and promote the welfare of children, and provide a safe learning environment
- Fulfil wider professional responsibilities.

(www.nurseryworld.co.uk/news/1175799,
accessed 18 April 2013)

A note of caution though; these positive initiatives are set against a background of, and have been affected by, the recent financial crisis. This has resulted in many local authorities cutting both training and bursary budgets. This has resulted in some local authorities moving from a situation where anyone who worked or lived in their area could access financial support up to EYTS level, to a current situation where in many local authorities this financial support has become available only to those staff in settings who have fewer qualified staff or are in areas of deprivation that qualify for support.

The current financial crisis has also had an effect on early years settings as parents struggle to meet childcare costs when their wages and jobs are affected. To date, and in response to the Nutbrown Review, the Government has responded with a bid to keep childcare provision costs down by altering staff–child ratios to make them more cost effective. This is a move that replicates an initiative in France and Holland where it was met with opposition from the early year's sector and also parents, both of who did not want to see what they perceived as a drop in standards for a cost-cutting exercise. As of June 2013 this proposal has been scrapped after opposition from all of the leading bodies in childcare.

Another financial restraint that affects staff in early years settings who are working towards higher qualifications other than level three, is the recent rise in university fees. Newly introduced is the extension of student loans to those in part-time education and this may be an option for some early years practitioners considering the arrangements for repayment. As of January 2013, to start a course in September 2013 a part time student would have to have a combined income of over £16,845 per household in order to have to make repayments on their tuition fee loan.

Finally the consequences of cuts in bursaries and raised tuition fees is in context against a profile of a sector of the workforce who have always struggled with low wages and the financial implications of what can traditionally be part time work. They share this profile with colleagues who are teaching assistants and after school play workers.

The raising of standards and training requirements are also set against a background of society's view of childcare and people who work in the sector. Bringing up the next generation should be rewarded with high wages and the best possible terms and conditions. Those working as practitioners at all levels will be aware that this is not the case.

Having said this, it is also clear that the profession as a whole has become more highly trained and more aware of what good practice looks like and how to achieve it. This awareness of high quality standards has been in place with the direct care that is given to children. It is now time to extend this good practice to the way that teams are managed.

The Plymouth serious case review

The guidance for settings regarding the leadership and management of teams has recently changed. The background to the recruitment and management of teams has to be the Plymouth serious case review that was carried out in March 2010 (www.plymouth.gov.uk/ serious_case_review_nursery_z.pdf, accessed 17 January 2013).

Overview

The review was carried out after images of a pornographic nature were found on the computer of a man who was later arrested and convicted. The images included those of a child wearing an identifiable nursery (Z) T-shirt. The nursery was closed immediately and an investigation ensued. During the course of the investigation it transpired that a member of staff (K) had been taking pictures of children in the toilets. That person was subsequently arrested and convicted.

The review's brief was wide ranging, as could be expected given the seriousness of the crime. It was charged with looking into all aspects of the nursery and of the agencies that had dealings with the nursery. The findings of the report were that no individual or agency could have foreseen the danger to children that K would present. However, it was looking critically at the leadership and management of the nursery to see if systems could have been in place that would have supported staff who felt uncomfortable with K and to provide an atmosphere where K would have found it hard to have the influence and the type of access to children that she did.

In terms of leadership and management the review was specifically detailed:

> To examine the recruitment processes carried out by employers of K where she was employed to work with children, to identify any gaps in vetting processes or breaches of recruitment policy (including for voluntary staff) and good practice applicable at the time.

The findings of the review make for uncomfortable but compelling reading and the review used language that clearly demonstrated the seriousness of the case and the subsequent urgency for change. It also showed that the issues that had arisen in the nursery in Plymouth had wider implications. The feeling from the review was that there were issues nationally and that additional guidance had to address this. When reading the review, nursery owners and managers were not encouraged to think, 'Well, that couldn't happen here'; far from the case, the language was hard hitting and gave rise to the feeling that the situation in Plymouth could happen anywhere. An example of the statements that the review made includes:

> K's power base within the setting and her capacity to draw other members of the staff team into her world, thus effectively silencing them, might have been more apparent had effective internal controls been in place.

And

> Z provided an ideal environment within which K could abuse. The lack of effective external controls, a setting where management was weak, and a blurring of boundaries across several

groupings resulted in a situation where the opportunity to abuse was available.

The review made many recommendations from its findings and those concerning staff management were that:

7.11 The Early Years Foundation Stage should require all Early Years settings to provide regular 1:1 staff supervision from a trained supervisor.

The message and recommendations that the review gave have been taken on board in the recent review of the EYFS and since been incorporated into the newly revised EYFS. The sections that relate to staff are in the welfare section and are:

3.18 The daily experience of children in early years settings and the overall quality of provision depends on all practitioners having appropriate qualifications, training, skills and knowledge and a clear understanding of their roles and responsibilities. Providers must ensure that all staff receive induction training to help them understand their roles and responsibilities. Induction training must include information about emergency evacuation procedures, safeguarding, child protection, the provider's equality policy, and health and safety issues.

3.19 Providers must put appropriate arrangements in place for the supervision of staff that have contact with children and families. Effective supervision provides support, coaching and training for the practitioner and promotes the interests of children. Supervision should foster a culture of mutual support, teamwork and continuous improvement which encourage the confidential discussion of sensitive issues.

3.20 Supervision should provide opportunities for staff to:

● discuss any issues – particularly concerning children's development or well-being;

- identify solutions to address issues as they arise; and
- receive coaching to improve their personal effectiveness.

3.22 Providers should ensure that regular staff appraisals are carried out to identify any training needs, and secure opportunities for continued professional development for staff. Providers should support their staff to improve their qualification levels wherever possible. For staff without a relevant qualification, providers should consider supporting them to obtain a relevant level two qualification.

OFSTED

The Plymouth serious case review clearly stated that the measures needed to ensure safe staff procedures were not currently in place in the EYFS and the revised EYFS addresses this in detail. This regulatory guidance is then followed up by OFSTED in their inspection process. How a setting is managed and led has a separate section in the evaluation schedule, an indication as to how crucial good practice here is seen as part of the effectiveness and safety of the setting as a whole. Good practice in leadership and management is seen as a crucial part of a whole setting approach to safeguarding children.

The criteria that the inspectors work to and make judgements on are:

When evaluating the quality of leadership and management, inspectors must consider the extent to which providers:

- fulfil their responsibilities in meeting the learning and development requirements of the Early Years Foundation Stage, including overseeing the educational programmes
- fulfil their responsibilities in meeting the safeguarding and welfare requirements of the Early Years Foundation Stage at all times, implementing them consistently to create an environment that is welcoming, safe and stimulating

- have rigorous and effective systems for self-evaluation that inform the setting's priorities and are used to set challenging targets for improvement

- have effective systems for performance management and the continuous professional development of staff

- have effective partnerships with parents and external agencies that help to secure appropriate interventions for children to receive the support they need

- how well practitioners and any trainees or students are monitored, coached, mentored and supported, and how under-performance is tackled

- the effectiveness of a programme of professional development arising from identified staff needs.

The evidence that inspectors are looking for includes,

The main evidence comes from interviews with the manager and/or registered provider or their nominee, supplemented by discussion with staff and parents and, if needed, sampling of policies and procedures. Inspectors should obtain evidence of:

- how well practitioners and any trainees or students are monitored, coached, mentored and supported, and how under-performance is tackled

- the effectiveness of a programme of professional development arising from identified staff needs

- the extent and range of completed training, including child protection and the impact of that training in improving children's well-being

- the effectiveness of the staff's monitoring and revision of the educational programmes to ensure that they have sufficient depth, breadth and challenge, and reflect the needs, aptitudes and interest of children

Current professional practice and policy

- the effectiveness of the monitoring of children's progress and interventions where needed to ensure that gaps are narrowing for groups of children or individual children identified as being in need of support

- the effectiveness of arrangements for safeguarding, including recruitment practices and how well safe practices and a culture of safety are promoted and understood

- how well required policies and procedures are implemented

- the effectiveness of self-evaluation, including contributions from parents, carers and other stakeholders

- whether well-focused improvement plans have been implemented through engagement with staff, children, parents and carers

- the effectiveness of arrangements for information sharing and partnership working with other providers, schools and professionals in order to identify all children's needs and help them to make progress.

(www.plymouth.gov.uk/serious_case_review_
nursery_z.pdf, accessed 7 January 2014)

Detailed on pages 17 and 18 is a summary of the possible judgements made about the leadership and management in a setting by inspectors and the terms that could be used about the quality of the provision in this area.

EYFS

Finally it is useful to look outside the specific standards around management and leadership. The entire requirements of the EYFS welfare and education standards need a skilled and motivated manager to lead a team in order to ensure that the setting meets the standards. It is not enough for isolated practitioners to work to the EYFS; the whole team must show how the setting in its entirety

Table 2.1 OFSTED judgements

Outstanding (1)	Leadership and management are better than good because: • Leadership is inspirational. The pursuit of excellence in all of the setting's activities is demonstrated by an uncompromising, highly successful and well-documented drive to strongly improve achievement, or maintain the highest levels of achievement, for all children over a sustained period of time. • The provider has an excellent understanding of their responsibility to ensure that the provision meets the safeguarding and welfare requirements of the EYFS, and has effective systems to monitor their implementation. • High-quality professional supervision is provided, based on consistent and sharply focused evaluations of the impact of staff's practice. An astute and targeted programme of professional development ensures practitioners are constantly improving their already first-rate understanding and practice. • Children's needs are quickly identified and exceptionally well met through highly effective partnerships between the setting, parents, external agencies and other providers.
Good (2)	Leadership and management are good because: • There is a good overview of the curriculum through monitoring of educational programmes to ensure a broad range of experiences to help children progress to the early learning goals. This is based on a good, secure understanding of the areas of learning and how children learn. • Planning and assessment are monitored to make sure they are consistent, precise, and display an accurate understanding of all children's skills, abilities and progress. Individual children or groups of children with identified needs are targeted so that appropriate interventions are sought and gaps are closing. • The safeguarding and welfare requirements of the EYFS are understood by leaders and managers and are met. Arrangements for safeguarding children are strong and well embedded. Clear policies and procedures are known and understood by all staff and implemented consistently. • Thorough self-evaluation takes into account the views of staff, children and their parents and is the result of careful monitoring, analysis and self-challenge. The drive for improvement is demonstrated by a clear and successful improvement plan that supports children's achievements

Table 2.1 OFSTED judgements—*continued*

	over time. Strengths and weaknesses are effectively identified. Planned actions to overcome weaknesses have been concerted and effective. There are strong links between identified priorities and plans for improvement.

- There are effective systems for performance management. Management and accountability arrangements are understood and consistently applied. Practitioners are monitored and under-performance is tackled. An effective and well-established programme of professional development is helping practitioners to improve their knowledge, understanding and practice.
- Partnerships with parents, external agencies and other providers are well established and make a strong contribution to meeting children's needs. Appropriate interventions are secured and children receive the support they need.

Satisfactory (3)	Leadership and management do not meet the grade descriptors for good.
Inadequate (4)	Leadership and managements are inadequate if one or more of the following apply.

- There is too little understanding of the learning and development requirements, resulting in poor monitoring of children's progress, particularly for individual or groups of children who are underachieving.
- There is ineffective monitoring of practitioners resulting in inconsistent practice and poor identification of training needs and/or practitioners do not have access to an adequate programme of professional development.
- There are one or more breaches of safeguarding and welfare requirements that have an impact on the safety and well being of children.
- Self-evaluation is weak and has too little impact. Any actions taken to tackle areas of identified weakness have been insufficient or ineffective. Providers are not sufficiently ambitious about improving provision and practice, including motivating staff.
- Management and accountability arrangements are not clear or are not understood by providers and/or their managers. Practitioners are not encouraged to improve their knowledge or practice.
- Links with parents, other settings or professionals involved in supporting children's care and education are not strong enough to ensure that individual needs are identified and met.

meets the welfare, learning and development needs of the children that it cares for. In this way the entire package of the EYFS must have as its foundation a well-trained and united staff team who are led and managed by a motivated and dedicated core team or individual. Without this there may be patches of good practice in the setting, but it will not form a cohesive unit that can deliver the highest standard of care to the children and families that it serves.

Observations

To look more closely at this and in order to give an example we can look at observation. Observation is a key underpinning part of practice in early years. It is only by observation that practitioners can establish where a child is, in terms of learning and development, what their needs are, what their interests are and if there are any safeguarding issues. Without skilful management, observations that are not focused and carefully recorded become bits of paper that are simply filed and not part of any ongoing assessment and recording process.

It needs the manager of a setting to establish what the methods of observations are going to be and consistently implement that as part of the settings practice. There are many systems that a setting can use and they all need careful consideration, discussions with the staff team and clear planning. The manager needs to make sure that there is time for observations and their writing up and that those observations are used as a tool to establish and track children's needs and development.

These observations can then contribute to a child's final profile, the document that leads them to year 1 and which requires at least twenty pieces of evidence to support the judgements:

> An EYFS Profile completed by the practitioner alone will offer only a partial picture of a child's attainment. Practitioners must

actively engage children, their parents and carers, and other adults who have significant interaction with the child in the assessment process. Practitioners may include the following to support their judgements:

- Knowledge of the child;
- Materials which illustrate the child's learning journey, such as photographs;
- Observations of day-to-day interactions;
- Video/tape/electronic recordings;
- The child's view of his or her own learning;
- Information from parents and carers; and
- information from other relevant adults.

> (http://media.education.gov.uk/assets/files/pdf/2/ 2013_eyfs_handbook.pdf, accessed 18 April 2013)

It should be apparent that in order to collect these different types of recordings the setting needs to be carefully and thoughtfully managed so that practitioners have opportunities for this and also time to pass the document onto the child's year 1 teacher and have a discussion about it.

Summary of the implications of changes for managers

From 4 November 2013, a judgement of 'requires improvement' will replace the current 'satisfactory' judgement for all early years providers – as it has already for schools and colleges.

Publishing the outcomes of the Good early years provision for all consultation, which sets out OFSTED's proposals for early years providers, Sir Michael Wilshaw, Her Majesty's Chief Inspector, announced that 'good' will be the minimum standard expected.

From November, pre-schools and nurseries requiring improvement will have a maximum of two years to get to 'good' – otherwise they face the prospect of being judged 'inadequate'.

(www.ofsted.gov.uk, accessed 6 August 2013)

The above is clearly a signal to early years settings that areas that are 'satisfactory' will need to be improved. This tougher approach is the other side of the Government's capitulation on staff–child ratios and demonstrates that they want to see proof of the way that a setting has implemented and taken on board the recent changes to the EYFS, and this highlights changes in the way that staff are managed.

Clearly managers need to see that these changes are not an option and that they need to look closely at what is needed for a setting to be judged as 'good' or 'outstanding' in their leadership and management procedures.

The most likely change that managers of settings will need to make is in the way that supervision and monitoring of staff is carried out. Good practice in this area will need to be either initiated if it hasn't been happening or checked for quality if it has.

Reflective points

After reading this chapter we suggest that it is a useful exercise to look at the OFSTED guidance for outstanding and good settings carefully in relation to leadership and management of the setting and to carry out an audit of where the reader's setting is in terms of achieving those standards.

Once the audit has been carried out (what is happening now) it is a good step forward to write an action plan to meet the gaps where the provision is not meeting those levels defined as outstanding.

Example of an audit

The starting point is to look at the OFSTED descriptions of what 'good' and 'outstanding' look like and to think honestly and clearly about the settings practice and if it could be described in those terms. When doing this it is useful to involve a range of staff. It might be that the manager of the setting thinks that their leadership and management meet those descriptions – does a more junior member of staff agree with this?

A suggestion would be to take two of the areas of leadership as below and think about three things from the list that could be put into action if they are not already happening. Both of these would make good topics for further discussion at staff meetings and/or between the core management team of the setting.

Management of placement students/volunteers

How is this achieved?

Is there a clear induction programme?

Is there a member of staff who is responsible for this area? Do they have time to meet with students' tutors/supervisors?

Are the roles and expectations of unpaid staff clearly discussed and agreed? Is the setting clear as to the helper's aims for their placement?

Do the children and parents/carers know who the students are?

Staff development and training needs

Who defines these?

Are they regularly reviewed at staff monitoring meetings?

Are both staff and manager clear as to who will pay for training and how the attendance at training will be monitored?

Does the setting have a clear policy on qualification training? Does it seem fair and equitable and agreed to by staff? For example what happens if two members of staff want to start a foundation degree and there is a limited budget?

Who decides the priorities for training needs of the setting? Does this match with practitioners' individual interests and needs?

This chapter has given an overview of the backbone of a setting; the standards that guide and form a setting and which have specific relevance to leadership and management, but are also all informed by the leadership and management of the setting. The next chapter starts at the beginning – how to recruit a team.

References

Department for Education (n.d) www.education.gov.uk, accessed 18 April 2013.

Department for Education (2013) Early Years Foundation Stage Profile Handbook http://media.education.gov.uk/assets/files/pdf/2/2013_eyfs_hand book.pdf, accessed 18 April 2013.

Department for Education (2013) 'More Great Childcare' www.gov.uk, accessed 9 June 2013.

Department for Education (2012) 'Nutbrown Review' www.gov.uk/government/ collections/nutbrown/review, accessed 7 January 2014.

Nursery World (n.d) www.nurseyworld.co.uk/news/1175799, accessed 18 April 2013.

OFSTED (n.d) www.ofsted.gov.uk, accessed 6 August 2013.

Plymouth City Council: Safeguarding Children Review Board (2010) 'Serious Case Review' www.plymouth.gov.uk/serious_case_review_nursery_z.pdf, accessed 17 January 2013.

CHAPTER 3

Recruitment

The success of a setting is largely dependent upon the level of
dedication, commitment and effort of the people within it.

(Blatchford and Manni 2007: 21)

Introduction

In this chapter we will discuss one of the most important decisions
a manager has to make – recruiting a staff member. It should be clear
by now that we think the team is the most valuable resource a setting
can have. It therefore follows that selecting a member of a team is
a crucial process. This chapter looks at the recruitment process from
shortlisting, interview and finally selection, making an offer and
induction. It includes some reflection points to guide the manager
and make the selection process more transparent and clear. One
important point to note is that this chapter refers to the 'owner' of
the setting. This is because it is the owner, who may be the manager
as well, who has the legal duty when carrying out employment
procedures. The manager could be the employee of the owner.

Legislative background

The whole recruitment process is structured and underpinned by
a number of factors. The first is the strictures of the EYFS welfare

and education guidelines. This means that selection of the staff member will be influenced by the requirement to have a certain proportion of staff that are qualified at level two or above. It may also mean that the selection process will be confined to applicants who have the post-graduate EYT status if the setting wants to have a higher staff–child ratio (see Chapter 2 for the legislative background to this). 'Ratios for three-year-olds and over were to remain at eight or 13 children per adult, depending on whether a qualified graduate was present' (www.bbc.co.uk/news/education-22782690, accessed 22 October 2013). Second, employment law is a further important part of the selection process. All early years settings have this double net of guidance and policy surrounding them: there are those frameworks that protect and care for the children who attend the setting, for example the EYFS and the Children Act 2004, and there are also the frameworks that protect the staff as employees. The Equality Act 2010 is the most recent legislation that owners of settings need to comply with. For example, it is illegal to discriminate against anyone who is on the 'protected characteristics' list:

- Age
- Disability
- Gender Reassignment
- Marriage and Civil Partnership
- Pregnancy and Maternity
- Race
- Religion or Belief
- Sex
- Sexual Orientation

(www.acas.org.uk, accessed 18 April 2013)

The Advisory, Conciliation and Arbitration Service (ACAS) website offers invaluable advice and support for anyone who is running a small business and employing a team of staff. It offers definitions and case studies of what constitutes direct and indirect discrimination, harassment and victimization. Owners of settings should also note that in addition to anti-discriminatory laws, it is also illegal to employ anyone who does not have a legal right to reside in the UK (Asylum and Immigration Act 1996).

Recruitment

Recruiting a team or replacing a staff member is an important part of the role of being a manager of a setting. While an early years provision may be classified as a small business there is no reason why the whole recruitment process – application, shortlisting and interviewing – shouldn't be treated seriously. There should be adequate processes and preparation from the manager.

We can refer once more to the Plymouth serious case review to illustrate the importance of this. As we noted in Chapter 2, one of the focuses of the review was

> to examine the recruitment processes carried out by employers of K where she was employed to work with children, to identify any gaps in vetting processes or breaches of recruitment policy (including for voluntary staff) and good practice applicable at the time.
>
> (www.plymouth.gov.uk/serious_case_review_
> nursery_z.pdf, accessed 7 January 2014)

It was found that there were no records of application or interview for K when she was appointed in 2006:

> There was no clear staff recruitment and selection policy and the manager had not attended Safer Recruitment training. K had been recruited via 'word of mouth' through the primary school, where the manager knew her in her school governor capacity.

Recruitment

> There are no records of an advertisement, formal interview or references for K's post, though there was a cleared CRB check.
> (www.nurseryworld.co.uk/news/1041189/Vanessa-George-Case-Review—Lessons-learned, accessed 7 January 2014)

It has to be stated that in the past some early years settings' employment procedures have been informal. Staff have been appointed on the say so of other members or because they have been working as a volunteer or parent helper on the committee, and other than the vetting procedures that have been legally required, i.e. CRB checks and health checks, other aspects of the whole employment process have sometimes been overlooked.

> I started working at the pre-school as someone left to go on maternity leave and I was one of the mums helping out. The then manager asked me if I would be interested in working one day a week on a regular basis and I started the next week.
> (Manager of a pre-school)

Starting points

There is online training available for people who work in schools to access safer recruitment training. If the nursery is part of a chain or managed by an organization, for example if it is owned by a university or NHS trust, then the organization's human resources team will usually manage the recruitment process as part of their role. For individual settings, most of those in the private and voluntary sector, they are classed as small businesses and need to initiate and manage their own processes. Online guidance can be very useful when considering recruitment procedures – see www.education.gov.uk/publications/eOrderingDownload/safer%20recruitment%20guidance%20-%20nov%202009.pdf.

The minutiae of every stage of recruitment would be too detailed to list in this chapter. Fundamentally, it is important that the whole process is efficient, effective and fair, in order to achieve the best result for the employer and the prospective employee. In summary though, there are key steps in the process:

- writing the job description and person specification and also establishing pay and terms and conditions of the post;
- writing an application form;
- attracting applicants – deciding where to advertise the post or set up procedures for an internal applicant;
- shortlisting from the applicants in preparation for the interview;
- setting up and conducting the interview;
- making the selection;
- following up references and checks (police and health), and establishing the validity of qualifications;
- making an offer;
- preparing for the new employee.

Job description and person specification

It is imperative for settings to have a written procedure and to give reflective thought to the way that they advertise, short list and select candidates for employment. As a basic necessity there should be a system for defining job expectations and measuring candidates against those expectations. This job-based criteria should be specific and ensure that qualified candidates are able to apply and be considered. This can be a valuable time to give reflective thought to what elements make up the job – what exactly is it that the successful candidate would be expected to do? What elements are not included in their role? It is good to think about how much responsibility they would have in terms of planning, liaising with parents and also other childcare professionals. It is important that both the setting and the candidate have clear expectations and understanding of the elements and boundaries of their role.

JOB DESCRIPTION: Pre-school Assistant
PURPOSE OF ROLE:

To provide a high standard of care for pre-school children in a stimulating environment which aims to provide Equal Opportunities ensuring that all legal, safety and individual requirements are met.

KEY RESPONSIBILITIES

- To ensure the children are cared for in a happy, safe and stimulating environment

- To have a sound understanding of children's developmental requirements

- To assist with planning, preparing and reviewing activities to meet the needs of all children

- To organise play facilities, set out attractively and supervise appropriate stimulating activities

- To assist in the preparation and cleaning up of activities

- To participate in observing and recording children's progress in order to maintain written records

- To liaise with parents and carers, act as key worker to a group of children, ensuring each child's needs are met

- To encourage positive behaviour by presenting yourself as a good role model

- To advise the supervisor of any concerns, accidents/incidents

- To adhere to the group's policies and procedures

- To attend meetings and appropriate training courses

- To ensure confidentiality at all times.

Figure 3.1 Sample job description.

If the package of tasks and responsibilities seems to warrant a vocational qualification, then thought needs to be given as to the level of this. Is this an assistant role or a supervisory one? Would a candidate who is currently training or willing to start training be considered suitable? It is important that vocational qualifications, if they are being sought, have evidence to show that they have been achieved?

The whole package of skills, qualities, experience and qualifications needs to be divided into 'essential' and 'desirable' criteria in the job specification. The manager must decide which items belong in which list so that candidates can demonstrate how they have met the criteria on each list. Try to avoid the temptation to put all the desirable criteria in the essential category; it is best to have approximately double the essential criteria in the list of desirables.

Reflection points

- Children need to see the world around them reflected in the people who care for them. It is a useful exercise to think about the diversity of the staff team in terms of age, race and gender.

- If there is a high staff turnover then before reappointing new staff it is good to think about why that might be. There might be issues about pay and work conditions that need to be adjusted.

Attracting applicants

Settings often advertise in the local press of the area in which they live. It is also worth investigating if the local authority has a jobs vacancy list for early years and play work. Here it is free to advertise and the manager can be sure that the vacancy list is going to people who are specifically interested in working in this field. Other places to advertise could be the local FE College or university who are running level three, undergraduate or post-graduate early years courses. There are also speciality magazines such as 'Nursery World'.

Shortlisting

Designing an application form is useful so that when applicants send or email their forms they can be easily compared and evaluated. Here the manager needs to look at the job role and specification and see if the applicant is able to meet the criteria. Those who have made the selection can then be shortlisted and be invited to interview. It is possible that unsuccessful applicants may ask for some feedback so it is good practice for managers to make some notes as to why particular people were not shortlisted and also what individuals could do to be more successful in the future. It could be that unsuccessful applicants may be suitable for a possible role in the future – for example, a baby room when at present there is a vacancy for someone for the rising school age room.

Reflection points

- Do applicants have suitable vocational qualifications? If not do they have any equivalent training and/or show a willingness to start training?

- What is their most recent experience? Would it bring a positive influence to the role that is being advertised? It is important to keep the particular role in mind and not just look at if an applicant is suitable for a generic post in the setting.

- What do other people say about their work? Have their references been included with the application?

- What are the absolute essential criteria? If it is to have level three qualifications and SENCO experience, then look through the applicants with this in mind and move out to one side all those who do not have this. Move onto the next essential criteria until there is a manageable amount of applicants to interview.

Interviews

Interviews are best carried out by more than one person. It makes the whole situation less intense for the candidate and provides an alternative point of view from the manager. It is important to have some time thinking and making notes on what is needed for the vacancy; the essential and non-essential criteria and what questions are most suited to gaining an idea of the candidates suitability for the post. After the interview it is important to make time to meet and reflect on each candidate in order to make a decision. There are useful ideas for conducting interviews online on sites such as www.inc.com/guides/2010/04/conducting-job-interviews.html, although many of them are more focused on the corporate workforce and need to be adapted for the childcare sector.

Structuring an interview

There are basic underpinning attitudes that need to be thought about when planning the interview. A positive way to look at the process is that the interview needs to be centred on drawing the candidate out and giving them the opportunity to feel at ease and to deliver their best possible performance. It is not an arena for catching someone out and trying to intimidate them.

Who should be at an interview?

There should always be more than one person. Who the other people might be is flexible. Three is a good number for an interview and this allows for a range of opinions for feedback and decision-making. In a pre-school this might be the supervisor, deputy and a member of the committee. In a private nursery it could be the supervisor, deputy and perhaps a member of the team who will be working with the successful applicant.

Starting the interview

There are some initial common sense arrangements: making sure that the seating is equal for interviewers and interviewees, i.e. that one is not positioned higher than the other, that all seating is comfortable, that there is water available and most importantly that the space is confidential and that you will not be interrupted. It may or may not feel appropriate to have a table between the interviewers and interviewee. It is a matter of choice as it can be useful to have somewhere to look at certificates and applications and to write notes on. On the other hand this may feel too formal and put off candidates.

> When I was interviewed for a part time assistant position I came to the church hall at the end of the pre-school session and sat on a chair at the end of the stage while the manager sat on the stairs, she towered over me and also I was aware of the tail end of other staff members leaving work behind me and the manager calling out to them but I couldn't look behind. I felt ill at ease and intimidated by the whole process.
>
> (Pre-school manager)

Initial questions

It is good to start with some personal talk to put everyone at their ease as they take off their coats and sit down. Introductions from all in the room and then questions about the interviewee's journey and the weather can lead on to talking about the interviewee's last post and their experience in childcare. It is important to establish professional boundaries here and personal remarks about the interviewee's appearance or personal circumstances – even if they are known – are not the right tone to strike for this interaction.

Further questions

Since the Plymouth serious case review there has been a shift in style of interview questions. Hypothetical scenario-based questions (situational) such as 'what would you do if . . .', have been replaced by actual experience-based questions such as 'can you tell me about a time when you . . .'. The difference is that the latter are more likely to reveal details about the candidate's moral values and actual experience. The former could just tap into what the candidate knows is an appropriate answer but has no further details to offer or discuss. The difference between these two types of questions was pursued in research conducted by Pulakos and Schmitt (1995), who compared the validity of two different types of structured interview questions (that is, experience-based and situational) under tightly controlled conditions. The experience-based interview questions required 108 study participants to relate how they had handled situations in the past, requiring skills and abilities necessary for effective performance on the job. Situational questions, administered to another group of 108 study participants, provided interviewees with hypothetical job-relevant situations and asked them how they would respond if they were confronted with these problems. The experience-based interview questions yielded higher levels of validity than the situational questions.

This might sound like a strategy to unnerve the candidate and in opposition to the point made earlier about getting the best from an interviewee. In fact, answering questions based on actual experience can provide the candidate with an opportunity to show their strengths and experience. Trying to second-guess what the interviewer requires with a situational interview question can feel stressful and worrying to a candidate.

The questions should also relate to the applicants suitability for the job and should be based on the criteria and the applicants' application. 'We need someone who can take a lead in planning the creative activities in the setting, can you give me an example of how you could do this?' relates to the criteria.

Questions that relate to the applicant's application are more likely to give them an opportunity to provide further details and show how their experience can be transferred to the vacant position. The most important thing is to encourage the applicant to talk and in this way give the interviewers material to base their assessment of their suitability on. This won't happen with 'yes' or 'no' answers. An example of this kind of question could be, 'you say here that you have had a lot of experience in running cookery activities for children. Can you tell me a bit about how you planned these around the children's interests?'.

Concluding an interview

It is important to thank the interviewee for attending and to give no indication at this point of the result of the process. A last-minute check that suitable contact details have been obtained is useful and it is essential to give applicants an idea of when they might hear the results of the employment process. If interviews have been conducted on a Friday then Monday afternoon would be an appropriate time to contact people. It is also good to establish how an applicant will receive the news and if they are happy with this. Will they be telephoned or emailed? Will this be followed up by a letter? Giving this news by text is not appropriate.

Making an offer

Once a suitable candidate has been selected they have to be informed and the setting needs conformation that they are willing to accept the post. This may lead to further discussions about pay and conditions. If these are protracted then it is a courtesy to inform the other candidates that the decision is in process with a general idea of when that may be concluded.

It may be that there is a delay in confirming references and qualifications and of course there should also be a CRB check and possible health checks as well. The job offer could end at any of these hurdles and it is good to inform the successful applicant that their take-up of the post is subject to all of these procedures being completed successfully.

Unsuccessful candidates may ask for feedback and with this in mind it is useful to keep detailed notes from the interview process, which can show why they have been unsuccessful and what they need to work on in the future. This feedback cannot be about qualifications or experience as these would have been made clear in their application and as a result of this application they have been shortlisted. The feedback needs to be about their performance at the interview or the greater experience of the successful candidate. It could be that the unsuccessful candidate wasn't suitable for this particular post, but that there may be future opportunities for them, in which case they are a valuable resource for the setting and contact needs to be maintained with them.

Induction

It is important to note that the appointment process does not stop after the applicant has started the job but that they should have a period of induction and support while the new member of staff becomes a valued team member. This induction should be structured and move from full support to the new team member working independently. The timescale for this should be discussed and agreed with the new staff member and also other team members around them, for example the other people in the room. A follow up interview should also be included with the manager as part of this process to assess how the induction is proceeding and any training needs that the new staff member may have as a result of the process.

> I didn't realize when I started at the nursery how much they used Makaton as an everyday tool and I quickly saw that I needed to get up to speed with this and go on a training course.
>
> (Nursery worker)

Reflection points for the follow up interview

- Has the member of staff been introduced to everyone – including part time staff and those who were previously absent?
- Are they aware of the policies and procedures of the setting?
- Do the parents/carers know who they are?

- Are they aware of the staff culture? (For example, we all have our own mugs, we buy cakes when it's someone's birthday)
- Will they be responsible for a small group of children? When?
- Are they aware of the planning and observation routines of the setting?

The next chapters will extend and continue by distinguishing between management and leadership of the staff team. Managing a staff team will also examine the embedding of a new member into a team and procedures such as monitoring practice and ongoing supervision.

Final words

The staff team is an early years setting's most effective resource. It follows that selecting a member of the team is an important job that requires care and consideration. The EPPE and REPEY studies found that effective settings where children made the best all round progress were settings where 'there was strong leadership and relatively little staff turnover' (Siraj-Blatchford and Manni 2007: 1). A wise and informed staff appointment that works both for the setting and for the individual will help with staff retention and preserve the feeling of continuity for the team and the children and families that use the setting.

References

Pulakos, E. D. and Schmitt, N. (1995) Experience-based and situational interview questions: studies of validity. *Personnel Psychology*, 48: 289–308. doi: 10.1111/j.1744–6570.1995.tb01758.x.

Siraj-Blatchford, I. and Manni, L. (2007) *Effective Leadership in the Early Years Sector: The ELEYS Study*. London: Institute of Education, University of London.

CHAPTER 4

Leading your team

Leadership is inspirational. The pursuit of excellence in all of the setting's activities is demonstrated by an uncompromising, highly successful and well-documented drive to strongly improve achievement, or maintain the highest levels of achievement, for all children over a sustained period of time.

> (OFSTED Evaluation schedule for inspections of registered early years provision, October 2013: 16)

Leadership is not something we do. It comes from a deeper reality within us; it comes from our values, principles, life experience and essence . . . leadership is a process, an intimate expression of who we are. It is our whole person in action.

> (Cashman 2008: 23)

There is a serious lack of leadership training for early childhood managers: it is likely that many are significantly under-prepared for this role. Research based on and drawing from the work of early childhood practitioners suggests that too often positions of leadership in early childhood settings tend to be held by 'accidental leaders' with minimal training to carry out their responsibilities.

> (Dunlop 2008: 7)

Introduction

This chapter explores how leadership is a distinct and important part of the early years manager's role. Leadership requires its own specific skill set and perspective. This chapter will consider what leadership is, the different aspects and styles of leadership, and offer practical examples of how the early years manager can develop this part of their role.

A leader or a manager?

Having considered the wider context and current policy for early years teams, as well as the process of recruitment, we are now turning to what happens next, once a team is established for a setting. Is it a team? Does a group of people all working for the same organization constitute a team? Bringing together a group of individuals with different personalities, ages, motivations and perspectives on life and creating an effective and cohesive, motivated team demands its own skill set of vision, social skills, organization and emotional intelligence.

Unpicking the roles and skills of the person who takes on such a task and heads up an early years setting is not straightforward. While there is much generally written about leading and managing teams and within education, very little has been researched and developed specifically around those working in early years settings (Moyles 2006; Muijs et al. 2004). More recent research and work by Carol Aubrey (2011) and Janet Moyles (2006) has begun to redress this shortfall and Moyles' ELMS typology (Moyles 2006) is one framework we have found helpful in exploring and bridging the gap between the distinctiveness of early years with general leadership and management theory.

ELMS typology (the Effective Leadership and Management Scheme for Early Years) was developed through research, review of literature and consultation with leaders, managers and experts and is 'a tool for all those who lead and manage early years settings that they can use for evaluating their effectiveness in the role of leader/manager' (Moyles 2006: 1).

The ELMS typology is presented as a tree with four main branches, each 'key areas that constitute effective early years leadership and management',

1   leadership qualities

2   management skills

3   professional skills and attitudes

4   personal characteristics and attitudes

(Moyles 2006: 12)

These branches are broken down and defined in more detail through further subsections of 'stems' and 'leaves'. These subsections highlight embedded 'qualities, skills, attributes, characteristics and attitudes' (Moyles 2006: 13) that grow out of the branches and stems. As a useful tool for scrutiny and evaluation this detailed framework provides a detailed and comprehensive map of the complexities of early years leadership and management.

While acknowledging and referring to the emerging debate and discussion in this area, our main concern is to provide signposts for those in early years so that they can better understand their own role and extend their awareness and potential for effective leadership and management of early years settings. We have decided to separate the strands of leading and managing and pull these two distinct roles apart, giving each a chapter of its own. This chapter will focus on exploring leadership and Chapter 5 will address the mechanics of managing. In our experience with early years teams, and those leading the teams, we have found that this primary and fundamental distinction is often unrecognized and rarely given the consideration and reflection that can significantly empower both those heading up the teams and their organizations. As an initial distinction for the difference between the two we see *leading* as focusing ahead on the horizon, knowing where you want to get to, and *managing* as the practicalities of organizing, training and monitoring to ensure you get there.

We begin by considering leadership for early years settings. What we mean by this is what can we consider to be the characteristics and markers of effective and outstanding leadership for early years teams.

Leadership starts with a vision

Individuals with overall responsibility for an early years setting are most frequently referred to as managers in the UK, although this does not adequately cover the range of multi-dimensional and multi-professional aspects of the job (Moyles 2006: 2). Reviewing a number of different journeys to early years leadership, Aubrey cites her own research as well as that of others, to illustrate how many practitioners do not have a clear career plan, transparent or easy to access framework or route for progression (2011: 78ff). Again, our experience working with a number of early years leaders confirms this; many find their expertise as practitioners with children leads them to a position where they are then also required to be experts at leading teams and working with adults – something completely different!

We start with being a leader because we see this role as pivotal in developing and sustaining an effective early years setting and team. We're going to begin by looking outwards, broadly and generally, at what good leadership is before refining our consideration to early years in particular.

In her extensive review of early years leadership, Dunlop (2008) refers to Solly's call for high-calibre leaders in early years who can maintain and enhance. These are obviously two very different roles and given the reality of early years settings today it is unsurprising that research continues to demonstrate that 'most leaders in early childhood settings in the UK found that roles common to their work could be described as focusing more on maintenance than development . . . more emphasis on management than leadership' (Dunlop 2008: 12).

So what is a leader? How do you know when you are being a good enough leader? In exploring this with early years colleagues we have found congruence with thoughts on leadership generally – namely that whether you are talking about early years teams or not, leadership is 'less a specific set of behaviours than it is creating an environment in which people are motivated to produce and move in the direction of the leader' (Horner 2003: 30). Illuminating this further, Jackson describes the role of the leader as 'to harness, focus, liberate, empower and align . . . leadership towards common purposes' (2003: xvi).

Much more than what a leader *does*, this highlights something deeper and more intrinsic, the kind of person an effective leader *is*. Here Jackson reminds us that equipped with a vision of where they want to take their team and organization, effective leaders have an important role in connecting with those around them to inspire, motivate and focus them towards the same, shared vision. To achieve this authentically includes the deeper underpinning values and ethos of a setting. For early years leaders this means knowing your vision and then being able to share that with your team and others in such a way so that it becomes their vision too; something that they also aspire to, own and share. To communicate, motivate and inspire in this way comes from deep within a leader; this is about passion, energy and knowing where you want to get to and be. The fundamental strengths and personal qualities of a person, who they are, is an important part of providing effective leadership. Cashman's unequivocal description of leadership, quoted at the beginning of this chapter clearly explains how this is integrally bound together in one person. Being a leader is inseparably and fundamentally part of who a person is. Just as our values, experiences, motivations, beliefs, strengths and what we see as our purpose make us the person we are, so does it create the kind of leader we can be.

Leading your team

With the pace and pressures of work and life many of the drivers and building blocks that make us who we are as people and professionals remain beneath the surface; unacknowledged and unrecognized. We suggest that a first and important step for leaders is to reflect on themselves and become more aware of their own values, beliefs, motivations and strengths in a more explicit and conscious way (see the end of this chapter for ideas on how to do this). There are two important and positive outcomes from doing this. One is that understanding oneself is a primary step in being able to better engage with and lead others – we have to know and understand ourselves before we can listen to and try and understand others. Second, by appreciating and bringing together their talents and values within a clear purpose, leaders not only know who they are, they can find more fulfilment, a clearer vision and be further strengthened by applying 'them consciously in a more powerful, tangible manner' (Cashman 2008: 62). The bringing together of these elements is described for leaders by Cashman as finding your 'sweet spot' (2008: 62). Once this core is better acknowledged and understood, a leader is then in a much stronger position to know and communicate their vision.

A leader's essential touchstone is a clear vision and they then need to have the people and team behind them to inspire and motivate to work towards that vision to make it a reality. A vision 'defines what or where the organization wants or needs to be' (Gill 2006: 98) and as such is a longer-term symbol of inspiration and change that can have the power to motivate and build a team with a common purpose and shared goal. Having a clear vision and being able to communicate that is a feature of effective leadership. It provides a point of navigation and clear statement about what a person stands for. From this vision a leader is able to challenge others by developing and creating meaningful and relevant norms, values and expectations for their organization.

This can sound like an unaffordable luxury in the pace and pressures of real life, however, we'd urge managers to rethink and reconsider. For it is vision that provides the *shared* purpose and motivation, the reason why managers and their teams do what they do. It is a framework for sharing goals, assessing where you are going, how you are getting there and prioritizing what is important for your team, your children and your organization.

Still stuck? When it comes to a useful vision the advice is to keep it simple, a statement of what you are trying to do (Gill 2006: 100). Simply stated visions are accessible and still have the power to challenge and inspire. Whether creating a new vision or reconsidering an existing one Kotter (cited in Gill 2006: 98) can help in offering six characteristics of a good vision:

1   imaginable

2   desirable

3   feasible

4   focused

5   flexible

6   communicable – can you explain it in five minutes?

An example of a vision statement is,

> We aim to provide a happy, caring and stimulating environment in which everyone has the desire to succeed and flourish.

A mission statement is often confused with a vision statement. There are no specific rules on this and they are often combined. A 'vision' includes the clear inspirational goals you would like to reach in the future. A 'mission' is how these goals will be accomplished through what you do every day. This can be seen in the following early years statement of vision and aims,

> The aim of [name] is to enhance the development and education of children under statutory school age, irrespective of race, culture, religion, means or ability. We do this by offering play facilities for the children and information sessions for parents as well as staff.

Leading your team

Once a leader understands and can articulate their vision, they then know where they want to take their team and organization. Crucially, a vision has to be articulated and communicated – it can't just stay inside a leader's head (and heart). Inspiring and leading a team means leaders have to have people behind them who are willing and able to follow.

Being able to effectively communicate a vision further extends the requirements and skill set of leaders. Communicating a vision effectively needs authenticity and so once again we are reminded of the importance of self-awareness and knowing yourself as key for leadership. Being an effective leader and being able to communicate a vision involves being able to model and live that vision, making the most of strengths as well as recognizing limitations; honestly acknowledging and facing up to this can often need courage and perseverance, along with a good dose of resilience, optimism and good humour. When leaders do this, the words they say have more power and impact because they have a purpose and come from who and what they are, what they believe in and what fundamentally matters to them.

Having established a vision that can be clearly communicated, the other piece here is the people it is being shared with. Here we move from self-awareness to knowing your team and your organization. Different strategies and ways of communicating that vision will be needed and shaped by the size and nature of a team. Communicating a vision is not a one off meeting; for it to be owned and inspiring for an organization, it needs to underpin and be woven into day-to-day routines and procedures. It is recommended that time is given to staff and other relevant stakeholders for a vision to be explored, discussed and agreed together as this promotes understanding, ownership, focus and greater motivation. This will need returning to and reviewing, particularly with staff turnover. It is important for leaders to remind and maintain this conversation and dialogue regularly so that it remains relevant and meaningful. Beyond verbal communication a vision can be reinforced and is powerfully communicated in the conduct of staff, towards each other, children and families, and how the vision is lived through routines, policy and procedures. These should all overlap and support each other and demonstrate practical ways that the setting is moving towards and living that vision. A vision is also communicated through visual reminders on display boards and on leaflets and websites.

Knowing your team and organization also has its own part to play in what kind of leader is needed at a particular time, something that itself needs flexibility and may change depending on circumstances and different situations. So having established the primary importance of a vision for a leader, what kind of leader is needed? How does anyone know what kind of leader they are?

Appreciating types and styles of leadership

Here our intent is to provide an overview and acknowledgement that there are a range of leadership styles and that an effective leader will employ a range of styles within their role depending on the situation. Being aware of this can help practitioners identify their own default style – as well as the areas they may neglect or avoid – and be more efficient in responding to and developing their team and organization. There is an extensive literature on types of leadership styles. While a long list of styles can be compiled (autocratic, bureaucratic, charismatic, democratic, laissez-faire and servant leadership, to name a few) a key distinction is often made between transactional and transformative leadership.

Transactional leadership focuses on supervision, organization and group performance, following existing routines and rules, rather than making changes. It is characterized by rewards and punishments as a way of establishing compliance from staff. This type of leadership is useful for emergency situations and delivering on specific projects. Transformative leadership incorporates the element of change and was first introduced by Burns in 1978 as a style where 'leaders and followers help each other to advance to a higher level of morale and motivation'. This notion was developed further in 1985 by Bass, who discussed transformational leaders as:

- role models who gained their followers trust and confidence;
- stating future goals;
- developing plans to achieve goals;
- innovating, even when their organization is successful.

This style of leadership has continued to gain prominence and attention over the last thirty years and has been noted as a 'dominant paradigm in contemporary British public sector organizations . . . particularly relevant for complex and complicated environments' (McKimm and Held 2009: 9). Bass and Avolio describe the four 'I's of transformational leadership as:

1 idealized influence – developing a vision, engendering pride, respect and trust;

2 inspirational motivation – creating high expectations and modelling appropriate behaviour;

3 individualized consideration – giving personal attention, respect and responsibility to others;

4 intellectual stimulation – continually challenging with new ideas and approaches.

Offering an additional perspective Goleman (2002: 70f) uses his research with 3,871 executives to identify six distinct leadership styles, each demanding its own underlying emotional intelligence for effective impact. We list them in the following table below, together with examples of how this could look in an early years setting.

Again it is worth remembering that there is no one right way to lead and the most appropriate and useful approach will depend on the skill level and experience of the team (knowing your team); the organization (knowing your setting) and a leader's own preferred style (knowing yourself).

Table 4.1

Leadership style	Explanation	What this might look like in an early years setting
Visionary	Moves people towards shared dreams, useful when changes require a new vision or clear direction is needed.	Doing something radically different to change direction of a setting. Being able to explain where the setting and team are going to staff and inspiring them to support and go along with you to make it happen.
Coaching	Connects what a person wants with the organization's goals, useful to help an employee improve performance by building long term capabilities.	When a member of staff is doing their job but is not performing at the peak of what they are able to do. Helping them to improve and get there.
Affiliative	Creates harmony by connecting people to each other, useful for healing rifts in a team, motivating in stressful times or strengthening connections.	Using staff meetings and out-of-work time to build relationships.
Democratic	Values people's input and gets commitment through participation, useful for building buy-in and consensus.	Working with whole staff team to address a difficult situation; seeking their ideas and solutions.
Pacesetting	Meets challenging and exciting goals, useful for getting high quality results from a motivated and competent team.	Useful with a high performing team for stretching them further and striving for greater excellence.
Commanding	Soothes fears by giving clear direction in an emergency, useful in a crisis, to kick start a turnaround or with a problem employee.	Preparing team and setting for an imminent OFSTED inspection. Arriving at work to find a burst water pipe and getting ready to open in one hour.

Sharing leadership

How leaders develop their team as leaders can contribute significantly to enhancing and developing an organization. This is because leadership is something all members of a team and organization embody. Developing a leader mindset across a team supports and encourages collaboration, focus and motivation, as well as fostering greater ownership, creativity and accountability between individuals (Arnander 2012).

A practical example of this is drawing on the contribution that can be made by EYPS staff, already discussed in previous chapters. Delivered across the UK since 2007, the EYPS is the graduate level professional accreditation programme for the early years sector, which focuses on producing not only highly skilled practitioners, but also individuals who can lead and support others. This is being replaced from September 2013 with the new EYTS. Practitioners who already have EYPS will not need to change their qualification. 'Early Years teachers will be able to work in all private and voluntary settings. Free Schools, new mainstream and alternate provision academies, and existing academies can employ teaching staff without the requirement for them to have Qualified Teacher Status (QTS)' (www.education.gov.uk, accessed 22 October 2013). Early years teachers will need to have the same entry requirements as those needed for primary teacher training but they will not gain QTS at the end of their course meaning that maintained schools will not be able to employ them as a classroom teacher. National evaluation of the EYPS programme in 2010 found that early years professionals 'were more influential on the quality of practice in their own rooms than on quality across the nursery ... [with] ... fewer measurable improvements ... in ... training for staff, and communications with parents' (Mathers et al. 2011). It would seem that while these higher qualified staff are having a positive impact within their own classrooms, in many settings they are an under-utilized resource for leaders looking to develop their settings and staff teams. We will return to considering other ways in which leadership can be shared in later chapters.

Before this, however, we are mindful that no aspect of this can be effectively carried out unless leaders first have determined their vision and are able to communicate it confidently and successfully with their team and organization.

A concluding paragraph on leadership

The recognition, call and need for high calibre leaders across all years settings continues to be voiced. Courses and leadership training opportunities, while still limited, are growing. However, with budget cuts and the increase of fees it is questionable how many potential leaders will be able to access this. We see the pathway to becoming a leader as most probably likely to remain relatively sporadic and as restricted as it has been for some time yet.

As we wait and hope for clearer and more supported pathways to leadership for early years, for those who find themselves in the role of a leader of a setting today we will consider other options for support, mentoring and training later in Chapter 8.

Reflection points

As a point for reflection we offer some questions to consider as you think about your own role, decisions, actions and responsibilities as a leader. Your agenda as a leader needs to include and focus on:

1   What personal strengths do you bring to your role as leader?

2   What aspects of your role as leader energize and motivate you?

3   Are there any areas of your role as leader that you do not give the attention they need because you are avoiding them?

4   How do you want your organization and team to look in five years' time?

5   How are you setting the climate for your organization?

6   What are the values that underpin how people treat each other and what you are focused on?

7   Does your organization know where they want to go and how they are getting there?

8   Think about how you are leading your team – what are you doing to maintain trust, include everyone, sustain effective communication and establish professional relationships and expectations across the team?

9   How are you building leadership capacity and including your team in a shared vision?

Many of these questions draw on those with primary responsibility in early years settings to be managers as well as leaders and so it is to the role of the manager in early years settings that we now turn.

References

Arnander, F. (2012) *We Are All Leaders: Leadership is Not a Position, It's a Mindset*. Chichester: Capstone.

Aubrey, C. (2011) *Leading and Managing in the Early Years* (2nd edition). London: Sage.

Bass, B. M. (1985). *Leadership and Performance Beyond Expectation*. New York: Free Press.

Bass, B. and B. Avolio (1993) *Improving Organizational Effectiveness Through Transformational Leadership*. London: Sage.

Burns, J. M. (1978). *Leadership*. New York: Harper & Row.

Cashman, K. (2008) *Leadership from the Inside Out*. San Francisco, CA: Berrett-Khoehler.

Dunlop, A-.W. (2008) 'A literature review on leadership in the early years', accessed online 21 April 2013 at www.educationscotland.gov.uk.

Gill, R. (2006) *Theory and Practice of Leadership*. London: Sage.

Goleman, D. (2002) *The New Leaders: Transforming the Art of Leadership into the Science of Results*. London: Time Warner.

Horner, M. (2003) 'Leadership theory reviewed'. In N. Bennett, M. Crawford and M. Cartwright (eds) *Effective Educational Leadership*. London: Paul Chapman.

Jackson, D. (2003) Foreword. In A. Harris and L. Lambert, *Building Leadership Capacity for School Improvement*. Maidenhead: Open University Press.

McKimm, J. and Held, S. (2009) 'The emergence of leadership theory: from the twentieth to the twenty-first century'. In J. McKimm and K. Phillips, *Leadership and Management in Integrated Services*. Poole: Learning Matters.

Mathers, S., Ranns, H., Arjette, K., Moody, A., Sylva, K., Graham, J. and Siraj-Blatchford, I. (2011) *Evaluation of the Graduate Leader Fund Final Report, Research Report DFE-RR144*. London: Department for Education.

Moyles, J. (2006) *Effective Leadership and Management in the Early Years*. Maidenhead: Open University Press.

Muijs, D., Aubrey, C., Harris, A. and Briggs, M. (2004) How do they manage? A review of the research on leadership in early childhood, *Journal of Early Childhood Research*, 2(2): 157–69.

Rodd, J. (2006) *Leadership in Early Childhood* (3rd edition). Maidenhead: Open University Press.

CHAPTER 5

Managing your team

The provider has an excellent understanding of their responsibility to ensure that the provision meets the safeguarding and welfare requirements of the Early Years Foundation Stage, and has effective systems to monitor their implementation.

High-quality professional supervision is provided, based on consistent and sharply focused evaluations of the impact of staff's practice. An astute and targeted programme of professional development ensures practitioners are constantly improving their already first rate understanding and practice.

(OFSTED Evaluation schedule for inspections of registered early years provision, October 2013: 16)

Introduction – reminding ourselves of an important distinction

For those leading and managing early years settings we have identified their diverse and complex range of roles and responsibilities. To effectively lead and manage in this role, leadership has been explored as the fundamental bedrock from which other roles and tasks can be performed. We have considered the key elements of leadership in early years and how this is knowing what and who you are, what you believe in and your vision, as much as what you do. If we describe effective leadership as knowing and being able to communicate your vision, then being an effective manager is about charting the course towards realizing that vision. The manager piece is focused on the practicalities, the reality of creating that vision. Both are needed for all organizations, including early years settings, to be successful and effective.

As a leader provides a vision to aspire to, it is the manager's focus on the short term and present that can make it happen in reality; setting up systems and monitoring to ensure all goes smoothly and that change is supported and sustained. If 'why?' and 'so what?' are the kinds questions a leader asks, then 'how?' and 'when?' are what a manager concerns themselves with (Lindon 2010: 158). Both leading and managing are complementary, carefully and intrinsically intertwined in many kinds of organizations, including early years settings, and often are found within the one person. One of the challenges with this is that the busy pace and range of day-to-day challenges can focus a person on the role of manager and simply getting by, keeping their head above water, at the expense of the broader concern and consideration of how they are leading their setting.

Crucial to getting the balance right is understanding what the roles of leading and managing are about and recognizing what is needed in different circumstances and situations within an organization. Once again we return to knowing yourself, your team and your organization as key to effectively leading and managing.

What is a manager?

For early years settings there is undoubtedly a significant overlap and need for both leadership and management. In this chapter we want to highlight and explore what an effective manager does. It can be inaccurate and unhelpful to sketch out hugely broad generalizations (Mumford 1993: 12), nevertheless there is plenty written and researched to describe what a manager does for organizations. In her literature review of leadership and management in early years, Moyles (2006: 4) describes management as involving 'control, direction, problem solving, planning, monitoring, resourcing, negotiating and doing'. Also refining their consideration to the specifics of what an early years manager does, Smith and Langston (1999) define a manager as someone who controls, does, organizes, accepts current practices, administrates, follows through, coordinates and is motivated by discipline.

More recently, in their Effective Leadership in the Early Years Study (ELEYS), Siraj-Blatchford and Manni (2006) highlight the effective leadership practices identified in the settings that took part:

- Identifying and articulating a collective vision.
- Ensuring shared understandings, meanings and goals.
- Effective communication.
- Encouraging reflection.
- Commitment to ongoing, professional development.
- Monitoring and assessing practice.
- Distributed leadership.
- Building a learning community and team culture.
- Encouraging and facilitating parent and community partnerships.
- Leading and managing: striking the balance.

For those administering this role we are sure managers themselves could add to that list! As discussed in Chapter 4, the balance between leadership and management is highlighted once again, although clearly this is a blurred distinction with areas of overlap. Given this long list of roles and responsibilities of a manager we're going to focus this chapter on managing in terms of three broad areas:

1 Managing practicalities and activities.
2 Managing relationships.
3 Managing yourself.

Effective managers in early years – three points to consider

Managing practicalities and activities

The day-to-day running of an organization requires a key person who can coordinate, plan, problem solve and make decisions. Given the pace and variety of demands within an early years setting it is easy to see how this can become the main way that managers spend the majority of their time. However, for effective managers it is not simply enough to cope with 'getting through the day'. Instead the role needs to include a proactive aspect (not just reactive and responding to whatever turns up). This proactivity includes holding of the vision and an ongoing movement towards it; a focus on improving and strategy; making the change happen; monitoring and assessing to check what is happening and how the organization is progressing forward. In addition to the mechanics of making the vision happen, the day-to-day practicalities of putting it into practice and progressing towards it, the further – and often more difficult – challenge for managers is addressing the necessary cultural change and values.

Changing professional practice and organizational change are key areas of concern for managers taking a vision forward and seeking to improve and develop their organization:

> One of the problems about learning from experience, of reviewing it, articulating it, registering what it means and improving it, is that it is always at best a secondary feature of what a manager has been doing . . . second by a long distance.
>
> (Mumford 1993: 4)

We'll continue to look at relating to staff and communicating clearly with them in later chapters. What we're concerning ourselves with here is the practicalities aspect – helping colleagues learn and change how they think, how they perceive their children and the organization, what they do and what they say.

The key ingredients for achieving this centre on providing the opportunity, time and encouragement for staff. Again we recognize how easy it is to offer such advice – in contrast to the reality of making it happen! Nevertheless making time for encouragement, conversations and identifying the opportunity and time to learn, sometimes getting it wrong in the process, is a proven way of making change that is sustained and embedded happen. Using experiences to understand, interpret and improve are an extremely effective way of engaging staff and fostering a climate of professional reflection and dialogue; all of which can be done at individual, small team and whole staff level. Making that happen, setting the expectations, creating the environment and asking the right questions – these are all how the manager can bring this about.

Staff meetings

Managing a staff meeting requires a particular set of skills that can be developed and might not be part of the usual range of a manager's expertise. Standing up in front of a group of people can be daunting, especially if the conversation is going to be difficult, and as part of their own self development a manager needs to think about ways that they can be more confident in this crucial aspect of their work. Some suggestions are:

- Presentation skills – these can be generic if special early years training is not available.
- Managing meetings.
- Developing consensus and making decisions together.
- Having difficult conversations.

I always felt sick with nerves before a staff meeting, especially if I had to ask staff to make a change to their practice. I had come from outside and many of the staff were older and more experienced at that setting than me. I knew there would be opposition to my ideas and one person especially would question the reason for change while others would just sit there with their arms folded and their coats on making it clear from their expressions that they didn't agree with me. After I went on training and learnt to breath deeply before speaking and other techniques for calming myself I felt much better. I learnt some phrases to say to help me contain the person who over contributed and encourage those who didn't more. I think the staff sensed the change in me and I got feedback that they were more confident in my decisions and less worried that I didn't know what I was doing.

(Manager of nursery)

Preparing for a staff meeting

This is covered in more detail in Chapter 6, 'When the going gets tough', as part of looking at what could go wrong or be difficult when leading staff meetings. We look at focusing on the purpose of a meeting, the space that a meeting is held in and involving staff in decisions. Chapter 6 looks at the content and the environment of a meeting, and there are also other ways that a manager as an individual can prepare themselves for staff meetings that need to be included in this chapter.

Body language and voice

As the case study above shows it is useful to anticipate what might be the reaction to training or news that the manager knows in advance will meet some resistance. The manager quoted above sensibly rehearsed some key phrases and calming techniques that gave them confidence. It is good to think about what would feed into and enhance this confidence and ensures that delivery at a meeting is the best and most assured that it can be. It could be something simple like wearing a certain outfit that is comfortable and doesn't have to be adjusted or cause problems when presenting. It could be that standing in front of the team gives confidence or that this is too difficult and that sitting in a circle is better. It is worth imagining the scenario and making adjustments until a perfect fit is found in terms of layout and how best to look in front of the team. For example if a manager knows that their hand shakes when nervous or that they can distract others by standing and fiddling then they need to think about standing and leaning against a table for stability or holding a folder to stop tremors.

Practicing different voice techniques to keep from revealing nerves is good; speaking slowly and clearly, breathing and drinking water when unsure or needing time to think before replying and regularly checking in with the audience to ensure that they understand what is being said are all techniques practiced by people who present regularly in front of groups.

Finally, when anticipating and playing out a staff meeting beforehand it is also good to keep a balance between positive and negative possible outcomes so that one is not overwhelmed by the thought of all the things that could go wrong but is keeping a realistic perspective.

Staff training – as a whole team and cascading

There are considerable difficulties around the reality of part time staff, split timetables and lack of time and money to pay for one-to-one supervision, whole staff team meetings and staff team training days. When considering this managers need to focus on the crucial fact that the most important resource that a setting has is the staff team. It is the quality of that staff team that underpins every aspect of the practice in the setting. The way that the staff team plan, interact with children, parents and carers and each other, carry out activities, manage observations and recordings, respond to change and observe statutory duties all depends on the team being highly skilled and motivated in their work and making time away from contact with the children for training is an important part of staff feeling that they are valued and respected as individuals and professionals by the management of the setting.

Whole staff training days provide an important moment in time for staff to reflect on and improve their practice. In a large setting it may be one of the few times they can meet and share ideas with staff members in different areas of the setting. Particularly valuable here is the opportunity to build a shared identity and understanding as a team together. Shared training together as a whole team enables a manager to clarify and establish a common understanding of practice and approach, including everyone in conversation and professional discussion. Good staff team training days also offer an opportunity for staff team building in many others ways that cannot be underestimated. With participation from the whole team in activities and discussion, and the chance to build relationships and trust, just the process of being together can support a team and organization in moving forward and embracing new ideas and change confidently and positively. With the possibility of establishing a deeper understanding, commitment and buy-in across the whole team it is a worthwhile investment of time that with appropriate follow up and support can ensure changes can be more fully embedded and sustained over a longer period of time.

It was an investment to have everyone together for a whole day of training and it is a big ask to get staff to come back together on a Saturday but they know that it is ultimately for the good of our children and they can take it as time owing . . . . Everything was great. I am so pleased . . . . This week I have been supported by them because they now understand what my aims are.

I recently had my OFSTED inspection and was recognized as outstanding . . . . Under leadership it says that the manager arranges training for the whole staff team – they really liked the photos on our website . . . *there* are two nurseries in my area with outstanding status and they are both mine. Very happy!!!
(Manager and owner)

The investment of time and money for whole staff training, while considerable, needs to be weighed up in terms of both content and process. The process of working and talking together brings its own benefits for team building, as does the content of your training, which, when delivered to a whole team, ensures that everyone gets the same message at the same time. Here staff training days can fulfil some of the functions of a staff meeting with careful planning. They can also release the staff meeting from having to cover cascading and feeding back on other training only a few staff may have attended.

Cascading and sharing training, while useful, is no substitute for actual attendance; hearing about training second hand in condensed form with some reprinted papers will never have the same impact for your team. Even with the best of intentions and high levels of motivation, those staff that did attend may not have engaged with the training, for whatever reason. It is possible that they may not have fully understood the training or be interested in it in the same way that another member might be, neither may they have the presentation skills to inspire colleagues once back to their setting. There are many factors that could simply mean that your staff reporting back may not be able to fully explain it, inspire or motivate staff once back at their setting.

The manager as helper

Exploring how managers support and enable staff to learn and change, Mumford (1993: 77) usefully explores the concept of help. Managers are often pressured and focused on getting the job done and short-term objectives. To achieve this they are usually reliant on colleagues to be flexible, adaptable and support them. In some situations managers are met with resistance and lack of cooperation. Because the role of helper is part of how many managers see themselves, Mumford's idea of help is useful in highlighting the need for managers to use very clear communication and to also be clear on what they are wanting for colleagues:

> Help is what a learner hears, not what a helper says . . . .
> Help is always defined by what a learner can accept and use, not what the helper can deliver.
>
> (Mumford 1993: 88)

Just being willing to offer help is not enough. Good managers know that what they as a helper can provide is also moderated by what an individual is likely to accept – 'to make a sale you need a buyer' (Mumford 1993: 109). We will move on to consider what we see as the most important aspect of being an effective manager – the relationship component: the success of any organization relies on the connection between people and how communication proceeds and progresses, or is blocked.

Managing relationships

As well as organizational skills and the demand for never-ending flexibility and adaptability essential for this task, the effective manager also needs to incorporate so-called 'softer' skills into their repertoire to truly have impact and develop their team and organization. Writing over twenty years ago Evans and Russell predicted a future that included rapid rates of uncertainty and change that they believed would need a new type of manager, where,

> handling such a future will no longer be a question of more efficient systems and structures . . . 'softer' management skills will become the new priority. The need for greater flexibility of thinking will become paramount. The organizations that will survive in the coming years will be those that are willing to let go of inappropriate attitudes and respond creatively to the pressures of change.
>
> (1989: xx)

In the same way as many other organizations, early years settings also require these less tangible, yet critical skills in their managers and leaders. While they were looking to the future, Evans and Russell were still able, even twenty years ago, to appreciate the growing importance of these skills; skills that require 'not just training but a much deeper understanding of ourselves ... [with] ... inner dimensions that are harder to see, harder to manage, harder to understand and much harder to handle' (Evans and Russell 1989: xxi).

In our work, from experience and conversations with many early years teams, what sets apart the ordinary from the good and the good from exceptional is relationships. It is the relationships that a manager builds, maintains and models with staff that we see as the key to not just the practicalities and activities highlighted above, but also the success of a setting more broadly. For many leaders and managers it is also most often the scariest and most daunting aspect of their role (see Chapter 6).

Its starts with trust

In Chapter 2 and throughout this book we will continue to refer to the fundamental importance of bringing a team together and sustaining a team of professionals who can work, focus and support each other. The higher levels of commitment and engagement that enable a team to excel are grounded in trust, between each other and with their manager. Although this is easily dented or even shattered, trust is frequently overlooked and left unattended. However, when noticed, nurtured and supported, then trust is the springboard for a team – and its manager – to flourish. In establishing trust a manager is more able to set and agree the boundaries and expectations for their staff as a team of professionals working with them and each other.

So practically what does that mean? We all have a sense of what trust is, even if that's gained through our experiences of *not* feeling able to trust someone. Articulating and consciously paying attention to trust is not easy because it is something that usually sits just below our immediate thoughts and day-to-day life. We are using the concept of trust to speak about connection, communication and relationships. In reality we're talking about a smile and hello, using people's names, consistency, mutual respect, fairness and listening as well as talking. Time together. All of these are tangible, concrete ways of building trust and the foundations for solid, professional relationships and dialogue.

Relationships help and empower effective communication

When trust is sustained and attended to in a group, those individual people have the potential to become a great team, with the confidence, resilience and motivation to support their manager, each other and the organization. Building these kinds of relationships with a team is not often easy and there are no shortcuts, but it is a worthwhile investment. Managers inevitably have to hold their staff team accountable to each other and themselves, asking staff to do things they often don't want to do, change what they do and how they think about something. Not only do managers have to get staff to do things they might not want to; they also need to support staff who may be stressed, struggling, demonstrating negative behaviours or not doing their job. To address any of these scenarios managers need to use clear, direct communication. Communicating effectively involves coaching, delegating, resolving conflict, setting clear objectives, providing feedback and valuing everyone. Underpinned with an ethos of trust doesn't mean it will just happen, but it does provide a solid ground to work from and talk together.

Giving praise

Sincere recognition and appreciation of staff is a further important part a manager's role and an essential element in a toolkit of managing relationships and being an effective communicator. There are a number of reasons why praise is important: staff who feel appreciated and respected are more motivated, committed and engaged; praise is another way for managers to build and sustain trust and positive working relationships with staff and it also highlights and reinforces good practice and behaviour.

There are some difficulties and pitfalls that managers need to be aware of though; while praise is important, its impact can get lost if those giving it want something in return, so it needs to be given freely and willingly just as it is, and not followed up with asking a favour! Similarly the impact can also be lost if praise is too over the top or too often.

Praise needs to be memorable and sincere, and this can be achieved by:

● being specific – say why rather than just commenting 'well done';

● doing it often – this will help staff understand what you are wanting from them;

● thinking of the person – some people prefer to be praised publicly while others prefer a more quiet word;

● including all your team – recognizing everyone's contributions and encouraging them all to flourish.

Managing yourself

The third area we want to highlight as a focus of effective managers is how they manage and organize themselves. Managers increasingly find themselves under stress with fewer resources, the complexity of supporting staff and the myriad of multiple demands both external and internal to their organization. These demands make it all too easy to be simply swept along with a never-ending list of challenges and situations to be addressed. Good managers learn to not just manage others, but also manage themselves, which means prioritizing and time management, as well as using effective communication to influence others, make decisions, negotiate and problem solve. We'll take a closer look at this in Chapter 8, for the purposes of our discussion here we signal it as an important aspect of the role of a manager in understanding the manager and leader distinction and for reflecting on your role as a manager and how effective you are.

Conclusion

The skills of a manager as a good communicator is fundamental to how they can engage with their team and take their organization forward. Managers are therefore encouraged to scrutinize how they communicate and reflect on how skills can be extended. Where communication is successful and effective, relationships are built and sustained and managers have a team around them where staff are energized and motivated, for their own personal satisfaction and for the good of the organization.

References

Evans, R. and Russell, P. (1989) *The Creative Manager*. London: Unwin Hyman.

Lindon, J. (2010) *Reflective Practice and Early Years Professionalism: Linking Theory and Practice*. London: Hodder Education (reader 2).

Moyles, J. (2006) *Effective Leadership and Management in the Early Years*. Maidenhead: Open University Press.

Mumford, A. (1993) *How Managers Can Develop Managers*. London: Gower.

Siraj-Blatchford, I. and Manni, L. (2006) *Effective Leadership in the Early Years Sector*. London: Institute of Education, University of London.

Smith, A. and Langston, A. (1999) *Managing Staff in Early Years*. London: Routledge.

CHAPTER 6

When the going gets tough

If a selection of early years managers were asked what worries woke them in the small hours of the morning, it is quite likely that it would not be issues concerning the care of the children, but probably difficult situations involving the staff team. These situations can sometimes escalate into disciplinary procedures and even further into dismissal. Managers can be ill equipped, unsupported and ill informed to manage and resolve such complicated and delicate proceedings. The lack of training in leadership in the early years (review carried out by Muijis et al. 2004) highlighted that 'there is a serious lack of leadership training, which could mean that many early childhood leaders are significantly under prepared for their role' (Moyles 2006: 2) and this can compound an already difficult situation.

In this chapter we aim to give an overview of the inherent and possible difficulties that make an early years workforce troublesome to manage and also some suggestions of ways to respond to difficult situations and prevent them escalating any further. We want to give a note of caution as in this section we are looking at times when systems break down. We are aware that this is not the experience of most settings and so this chapter attempts to support managers in extreme situations and also provide material for others to prevent events escalating to crisis point. We are not intending to sound negative about early years provision, but to realistically acknowledge the difficulties and problems that are inherent in managing any team of people.

A working environment that is physically and emotionally predestined to create tension and problems when there is conflict and dispute aggravates the lack of experience and training in dealing with these issues.

Reasons for difficulties

Space

Physically, many early years settings have problems in having places where staff and managers can talk confidentially, to each other and also to parents/carers and other professionals. When planning the space and allocating areas in settings the focus is on the children's needs. This is of course understandable and in line with OFSTED welfare requirements. It can however, mean that interviews with staff members happen in the space that is left over when the children's areas have been allocated. In a building that has not been purpose built for the setting this can cause difficulties. In the recent Government paper 'More Great Childcare' (January 2013) there is reference to having a confidential space in a nursery as desirable but not essential. In fact, being able to talk privately with staff and also parents and carers, away from interruptions, is a crucial aspect of running a setting.

As a local authority and OFSTED inspector I saw a range of areas that were for staff use. They ranged from cold and unused rooms in the back of church halls – spaces that were enlarged stock cupboards with no natural light – to rooms that served as a combination of office, a place to eat lunch and a kitchen/laundry room. There was mixed understanding of the term 'confidentiality', and it could be hard to have a discussion without being interrupted. This was difficult if I needed to have discussions about members of staff or interactions with children that I had seen.

If a common area is reserved for these discussions then it can deprive staff members of a place to have a break or to write up the observations or notes from their work with children while they are fresh in their mind.

Time

Many early years settings are privately owned and treated as commodities where the parents are the consumers of the product. This can result in staff hours relating strictly to the time that is worked directly in contact with children and so time for extra planning, meetings and other non-contact time activities are sometimes not paid for. Because many day care facilities are open 8am – 6pm all year round and rely on shift rotas there are few times when staff can get together to have whole group discussions. Sometimes staff are expected to stay on at the early years setting in their own time to attend important briefings and updates. Because of local authority financial restrictions it is rare for settings to be externally funded to release staff for training, indeed in addition such training is now often paid for by the setting. Because of this many settings will just send one member of staff to training sessions with the expectation that they will then cascade the information they have gained to the whole team at a future staff meeting.

This in itself is not ideal, as every staff member would have a different experience of a training session depending on his or her aptitude and interests and so to relay this to others can be difficult. For the staff attending training, a session might have seemed uninteresting and not relevant to their work. To another staff member, with a different age group and working in an alternative environment, the training could have been enriching and motivating. It is also true that not every staff member is confident or adept at sharing information and so their rendition/cascading of a session that they have attended could fall short of transmitting the original intent of the trainer.

When the going gets tough

As a result of this information sharing, already infrequent staff meetings have overcrowded agendas and staff are reluctant to fully debate and discuss items in order to get through the whole programme and finally finish the day.

The consequence of this is that the core management of the setting – the manager and deputy perhaps – have to make crucial decisions away from the team. This can result in the team feeling that they haven't been consulted and so not fully supporting any changes.

> In my setting the staff meetings were hard to organize and when they happened were infrequent and short. As a result I used to meet with the deputy afterwards and we would make decisions on items that there was no time to discuss and present them to the rest of the team at the start of the next meeting. I thought we were saving time but although the practitioners said that they agreed with us at the meeting, afterwards I could sense through gossip and also a sense of the atmosphere that many of them hadn't really agreed with us. This escalated into a sense of 'them and us' that I found really upsetting. After all, we were only doing this in order to save their time!
>
> (Nursery manager attending university leadership course)

This is, of course, a worst-case scenario and there are many settings that are not under these kinds of constraints and have made more suitable arrangements. The above is to illustrate how communication can break down because of physical and time constraints.

Attitude

In the same way that space and time are organized to prioritize the needs of the children attending the session, the ethos and underpinning values of the practitioners are focused on working with children. We are not suggesting for one moment that this is an inherent difficulty, but want to identify possible problems with this stance. People are drawn to work with children for a range of reasons; they may have a strong sense of vocation and have always wanted to work with children, they may feel that they have the skills and experience of caring for their own children and this equips them for early years work or they may regard this work as a stepping stone towards other work when they have more qualifications or have less caring responsibilities.

Whatever the reason, one thing that they are focused on is that they will be working with children. Most people do not go into work with children because they particularly want to have contact with adults, but in fact that will be a large part of their work. From having contact with other team members, to meeting with parents and carers and liaising with other childcare professionals, effective working and communicating with adults is central to maintaining best practice in this kind of work.

This kind of communication demands a range of skills that may be unfamiliar to early years practitioners – assertion, presentation, negotiation, team involvement and taking part in meetings. We talk more fully about accessing these skills as a manager in Chapter 8 and how they can help shape the purpose and vision of the managerial role. If this is unfamiliar territory to practitioners, then when faced with difficult situations where they feel misunderstood, undervalued or unheard, they may retreat to a range of behaviours that are unhelpful and can also exacerbate a situation. This may include agreeing in public but not acting in accordance with this, gossip in the staff team, passive aggressive behaviour that quietly undermines practice, avoidance of situations that make them feel uncomfortable – such as not meeting with parents or seeking help for a child that may bring them into contact with people who would question their current practice.

In addition to space, time and attitude, Rodd (2006) notes that early years teams also have other physical difficulties. The groupings of nurseries into different rooms and working shifts to cover extended opening hours can mean that communication is affected as staff can be relatively isolated in rooms and at the beginning and end of days. Having the workforce grouped in sub groups in rooms can also affect team spirit by staff forming allegiances to their rooms – the toddler rooms and baby room for example. Also,

> the fact that two or three staff members can be required to work closely in relative isolation from other staff can lead to mis-perceptions of favouritism by the team leader, resentment about imagined benefits or privileges that staff in other rooms might receive and rumours about team leader's attitude to performance in the various rooms teams.

> (Rodd 2006: 107)

Supervision difficulties

Ways to manage difficulties

Assertion techniques are an essential tool when dealing with the demands and expectations of others. By modelling this good practice the manager is also showing the staff examples of respectful and professional interaction. Dedicating a staff meeting to laying out the principles of assertive behaviours is a good way of ensuring that all staff at least have a baseline understanding of assertion and an ultimate goal when thinking about their day-to-day, adult-to-adult relationships.

As an aside it is also good for the children and parents/carers to have awareness and see examples of the adults managing and working in the setting, responding to each other with respectful interaction.

Case study

Problem situation

Elly, the manager of a nursery, is becoming increasingly frustrated as Jess, a room leader in the toddler room, is constantly late in the morning. Everyday there is a different reason why she is late, and by the time Jess is ready for work Elly has had to set up the equipment and prepare the children's space on her own. The other two members of staff are timetabled to start at 8:30am and Jess has specifically asked for the early 8am shift so that she can leave early.

What Elly could do and what might happen

She could say nothing in response to Jess's apologies and seethe in silence. If she does this the other staff will pick up on the tension when they come in and the atmosphere is likely to be transferred to the children causing an unhappy and tense environment. She could have a row with Jess and shout at her, telling her off for her lateness and saying that Jess is causing stress to her, Elly. If she does this it is possible that Jess will be very upset and tearful or she may be defensive and argue that she is not causing a problem and retaliate with shouting as well. Either way, when the staff and children come into the nursery there will be an atmosphere and unresolved upset. These two responses are low and high on the emotion scale. The first one is called 'passive aggressive',

> Passive aggressive behavior is the term used to describe behavior that is passive in expression but is aggressive or malicious in intent. The purpose of passive – aggressive behavior is to express anger without having to be responsible for that anger, so anger can be denied.
>
> (Bacal 1998: 36)

75

When the going gets tough

It is often the response of someone who is unsure how to access their feelings and is worried about the responses they might get in return if they are vocal about how they feel.

The second response is aggressive behaviour. In the workplace there are bound to be times when conflict arises. Staff members will occasionally get upset and angry and may snap at each other. This is not ideal behaviour, especially if it happens in front of children. However, isolated incidents do occur and should be resolved as quickly and calmly as possible. The people involved need to feel that any residual anger or upset has been expressed, they have discussed the incident, it is dealt with and that they can resume a cooperative and professional relationship.

This second response from Elly will certainly upset and undermine Jess and if Elly continues over time to express her frustration with Jess's behaviour in this highly charged way she could be seen as bullying Jess and instead of being the person who is trying to deal with a member of staff's unprofessional behaviour she is answerable for her own inept handling of the incident.

The assertive technique

When Jess comes in Elly works with her to set the room up and lets Jess know that she needs to speak to her later about her lateness. As soon she can Elly has a private interview with Jess. During this time she says that she has been keeping a record of Jess's lateness (*this is what has happened*) and that she feels frustrated that it has happened so often (*this is how I feel*). They then have a discussion about strategies to stop it happening in the future and make a resolution, possibly for Jess to come in later and have a shorter lunch break, so that she can still leave early (*this is what I want to happen in the future*). Elly also talks about the consequences if it still happens (*formal warning perhaps*) and sets a date for the situation to be reviewed.

It may be that Jess finds it hard to relate to such a direct approach and starts to become upset. In this case Elly can be supportive and understanding but make it clear that the situation has not been resolved and when Jess feels calmer and more able to talk then they will have to resume the discussion. Elly can also talk about the things that she values with Jess's work and the strengths that Jess brings to the team.

This is the three-step assertion technique – saying what has happened, how it makes the person talking feel ('I' statements help establish a non accusatory area) and what they want to happen in the future. The techniques need practice and it is useful for a manager to practice them outside the workplace, for example when making a complaint about goods or services. See this website for an example of how this interaction may proceed – http://therapy-now.com/assertiveness-techniques.php. The three-point plan is a very effective technique and one that helps establish and maintain clear and honest relationships.

As with any change of behaviour it can be resisted by others who may see assertiveness as being aggressive. By keeping calm and making lots of 'I' statements the manager is modelling a style of interaction that is professional and open and ultimately works with the team member to solve a problem.

Defensive behaviour

The case study sets out a situation where the responses lead to a solution. Inevitably there are times when this does not happen. It is good for the manager to remind himself or herself that they can only define their own behaviour and not others and that the other people in the situation make a choice about how they want to behave. If the staff member is being defensive in their actions, *'Why should I be picked on, lots of other people are late in and they don't get into trouble?'*, then a useful technique is to ignore the attempt to get onto other territory (that is, the behaviour of others) and to stay focused on the issue, *'What is the main reason why you aren't able to get here on time?'*

When the going gets tough

The manager can, by modelling this assertive behaviour, give the other person room to be able to cooperate and respond honestly without having to defend their position and escalate the conflict. Having a three-point plan can seem like a mechanized response to an emotional situation. It is not our intention to suggest that the manager needs to have an identical 'script' that they use to respond to every situation. Within the plan there is a need for the manager to interact with others as an individual and also show that they are an understanding and concerned practitioner. That understanding and concern needs to be genuine, not assumed in order to get to a solution. The baseline is that both of you are trying to reach an agreement in the best interests of each other and ultimately the children and other users of the setting.

Staff meetings

This is another possible area of difficulty for the early years manager. It is useful, in order to maximize the strengths of the staff meeting, to first think about the purpose of them. Why are the staff gathering?

Purpose of meeting

1   To have a briefing – to listen to updates in policy and/or changes that you need to give them. This can also include a cascade of information from various trainings that the manager or other members of the staff team have been on.

2   To have a discussion – this involves posing a problem or area of potential change to the group and receiving their thoughts and feedback through a facilitated discussion.

3   Staff training – to lead a training session for staff.

4   Team building – to carry out activities that bring the team closer together and working more effectively as a unit with a shared purpose.

It is important to make the purpose of the meeting clear and to convey this to the team. In this way there is less likely to be a mismatch of the manager and the teams' expectation of how the time will be spent. If staff feel that they are making special arrangements to attend meetings that are out of their working hours and when they are not able to contribute, but merely to listen, then it can lead to low morale. Staff teams can easily feel that they are there just to 'rubber stamp' the decisions that the manager and deputy may have made in advance. Feeling estranged from the decision making process and so disempowered can result in staff removing themselves from feeling part of the team and identifying themselves with the setting.

This can lead to problems such as staff forming small cliques who voice discontent in a passive aggressive way and gossip with each other, or individual staff members who outwardly agree with change but do not take it into their practice as they have not felt part of the process of arriving at the change or simply do not fully understand it.

> The meetings happen once a term and I try and give the agenda out two to three weeks in advance of the meeting so that everyone is aware what will be happening. We use the meetings for a mixture of briefing on changes, deciding training needs, discussing any problems and a social as I always provide food and have them at my house. Staff can have items on any other business and discuss with me beforehand if they want to raise anything.
>
> (Pre-school manager)

Practicalities

When will the meeting be held?

Terms and conditions of staff vary between settings and the basis on which staff attend meetings needs to be made clear to them.

Will they be paid for this time? Will they be able to attend? The manager needs to be aware of the needs of staff in terms of giving up time that they are not being paid for and has to think about staff childcare commitments and other demands on their time. Even if staff are being paid for their time they may not all be able to attend. Informing them well in advance of any meeting makes it more likely that staff can arrange to be there. If important decisions are being made at the meeting it is imperative that staff are there in order to receive the information and be part of the process.

Where will the meeting be held?

It may be easiest to have it at the setting but this is not always possible if the space is a shared one (like a church hall). Wherever it is held it is important that everyone is comfortably seated and can see and hear everyone else. At the end of a long working day staff will be tired and it is good to ensure that there are refreshments available for them. Meetings should start and end on time and the agenda should not be overloaded. Items on the agenda should be listed in priority. It is not good practice to have a crucial decision made at the end of the meeting when people just want to leave and may be already getting their things together in preparation. The manager should manage the time so that the end of the meeting can be completed in a purposeful manner and they can sum up any important decisions made and end on a positive-looking-forward note rather than being rushed.

Skills for meetings

It is good at this point to refer back to Chapter 5 and the ideas for improving the skills for the team and the manager in meetings. Leading and being in a meeting are skills that practitioners can learn. Meetings can be improved if both managers and teams are able to listen attentively, take turns in speaking, contribute without fear of ridicule, speak honestly and openly – in fact all of the behaviours that the early years worker would want to foster in children are ones that as adults need to be modelled.

What can go wrong

The issues that early years managers often discuss when talking about the 'staff meeting from hell' are around:

- One member of staff dominating the meeting while others sit and don't contribute.

- An overcrowded agenda that means the meeting overruns and some staff leave.

- So much social 'chit chat' and mingling that it is hard to focus on the business at hand.

- Staff confronting each other in public.

- Inexperienced managers not being able to manage the meeting or respond to questions.

We hope that the material in this book will help managers not only to be more effective in managing staff meetings but also to share the responsibility by engaging the team around the concept of being an active participant in a meeting and seeing it as a valuable part of their practice. The concept below of 'restating the obvious' might be helpful in these cases.

Restating the basic position

This is a technique that can work on a one-to-one basis or with a whole group in a staff team. It is about making a statement about why you are all working at the setting. The manager could, at a staff meeting, go round the whole team and ask all the practitioners why they are working at the setting or what they think are the core values of a team member. The expectation is that there will be useful discussion about the shared values that they have, for example, that they all have the well-being and development of the children in their care at the forefront of their practice.

The manager can also use this restating of values with an individual team member. In the case of Elly and Jess that we considered earlier, Elly can use this exercise to show Jess that they are both working at the setting for the same purpose. They have shared ground with the same focus even if they differ in how this focus needs to be carried out. It can provide a starting point for agreed discussion and is a respite of accord after dispute. Of course, this shared vision is also influenced by how the practitioners see themselves. Moss (2006) discusses three possible visions of the early years worker; as a substitute mother, a technician or a researcher. He goes on to state:

> Ideas about children, as well as about parenthood, are changing too. Constructions of children as knowledge reproducers and redemptive agents, who require shaping and processing by technicians, do not sit comfortably with constructions of the child as an active subject, citizen with rights and co-constructor of knowledge, identity and values, while maternalist assumptions, with their upbringing norms, can and do change over time.
>
> (2006: 39)

The aim of the setting should ultimately be that the practitioners see themselves as valuable professionals who are able at their job and have a set of skills and knowledge that they are constantly replenishing and enriching. With the adults around them having this self-confidence and pride in their work then the children are also able to be active and independent learners who are able to express their feelings and work cooperatively with the adults around them and the other children in active exploration of their world.

This discussion of shared values can start to bring about cohesion. It can bring with it an understanding of how practitioners may have differences in the means by which they achieve core values; but that these values are central and embedded in all of their practice and understood and agreed by all. It makes a starting point on which agreement has been reached and is a powerful tool that the manager can use to start to bring together a discordant or troubled team. It can be the foundation stone in the process by which a team can start to negotiate and define the vision of the setting and all adhere to its precepts.

References

Bacal, R. (1998) *Conflict Prevention in the Workplace: Using Cooperative Communication.* Winnipeg, Canada: Bacal.

Moss, P. (2006) Structures, understandings and discourses: possibilities for re-envisioning the early childhood worker, *Contemporary Issues in Early Childhood,* 7(1).

Moyles, J. (2006) *Effective Leadership and Management in the Early Years.* Maidenhead: Open University Press.

Muijs, D., Aubrey, C., Harris, A. and Briggs, M. (2004) How do they manage? A review of the research on leadership in early childhood, *Journal of Early Childhood Research,* 2(2): 157–69.

Rodd, J. (2006) *Leadership in Early Childhood* (3rd edition). Maidenhead: Open University Press.

CHAPTER 7

The wider community

Children's needs are quickly identified and exceptionally well met through highly effective partnerships between the setting, parents, external agencies and other providers.

(OFSTED)

Understanding the role of the wider community for early years managers and leaders

An early years setting does not exist in a vacuum, neatly packaged and sitting in its own isolated bubble. Real life is much messier and when it comes to leading and managing early years settings, a manager has to prioritize relationships and connections with others outside of their four walls, as well as what is happening within them. In this chapter we will be exploring the diverse range of external connections, relationships and partnerships that are integral to early years good practice, as well as the different ways managers can establish and maintain these relationships as a fundamental part of their role as leader and manager.

Each early years setting inevitably has its own unique map of how it is situated within its wider community and area. While a manager's map will be specific to their own geographical area, location, cultural and social environment, there are common features and landmarks that are useful to recognize and utilize when positioning a setting and understanding the external dimensions to the role of leader and manager.

The two-way street of a wider community

The wider community has an important role for a manager, their organization as a whole and for the specific needs of staff and individual children. Multiagency working is one aspect of this and it forms an essential part of the manager's role, particularly in the arena of child protection and child welfare. However, the wider community is more than just working with other agencies; parents, carers and families are another immediate way that settings reach out beyond their immediate setting. With a broader outlook, further connections and associations can be a valuable and enriching way of supporting and developing a setting.

None of these links are a one-way relationship; instead the most useful and beneficial connections are characterized by dialogue, conversations and mutuality. We see these elements as the foundation for how effective and outstanding early years settings establish and locate themselves within their wider community. What we are encouraging leaders to consider here is not just who is my wider community, but also, *how* am I and this setting an active and integrated part of this community? As we move on to unpick the different ways settings can connect with their wider community it is mutuality that we want to foundation our discussion within. As we explore the various ways of linking with the wider community we will focus on who this is and how those links and mutuality can be established, sustained and developed.

Who is out there? Who to connect with?

So who is out there? We want to provide managers with some obvious answers as well as other ways of considering broader opportunities and connections. While our suggestions and mapping can only be a general picture, we recommend managers use this chapter to note and map out their own community links. We'll offer some ideas of how to do this at the end of the chapter.

Your organization – the community close to home

The setting's foundation

Early years settings have a variety of different foundations ranging from church based, local authority owned nurseries, nurseries managed by universities or medical trusts, private settings or linked to schools. The foundation status determines the intake of children as well as how a setting is held to account and overseen. Whether overseen by a board, governors, trustees or committee, these are crucial relationships. It is one of the key ways managers are held accountable for what they do in their role as leader and manager. It is important therefore that both parties are clear on the expectations and parameters around this. Managers are advised to check out and be clear on their terms of reference and how roles and responsibilities are agreed. They should also be clear on how often and what kind of level of detail is required for reporting. Managers will have their own vision and plan for developing their teams and settings; gaining the support and understanding of those overseeing this helps enormously so it is advisable to maintain frequent and clear communication – this can offer managers valuable personal support and advice, as well as ensuring that the setting as a whole benefits as an organization where everyone is working towards the same vision and goals.

While this is a formal structure, more informal dialogue is often an additional feature of this particular wider community link. As we noted earlier, when looking at building relationships within your staff team, the same principles of attentiveness to building trust and maintaining clear communication, as well as maintaining the boundaries of professional dialogue, are all effective ways of ensuring and sustaining positive partnerships with those who oversee managers and the setting.

For those working within a privately owned setting it is still good practice to liaise with the local authority children's workforce team, although as we write this it is currently under discussion at government level and could change any day.

Your families

The other immediate group that any early years manager must engage with and continually seek to maintain positive relationships with is parents, carers and families of the children at their setting. Knowing parents and carers is essential for finding ways of maintaining communication and ensuring concerns, issues and questions are able to be raised from both sides. Language, mobility or unfamiliarity with formal systems of care can prevent families from engaging in or understanding routines and conversations about their child. For settings that have a proportion of working parents, children are often collected by other family members, child-minders or other carers, and this can mean less face-to-face informal contact. In these situations, more creative ways of staying in touch and maintaining communication need to be considered, for example by using email, an up-to-date website and text updates.

The profile of families, parents and carers for a setting can also require careful regard for session times. In an area of deprivation and unemployment, the demand is most likely for more part time places and flexible sessions. In a commuter area, with a larger proportion of working parents, families are more likely to welcome earlier opening times and later closing. For larger settings, school holiday care could be more appropriate for siblings.

Children thrive and cope better with parental and family support. Other opportunities for helping families develop an active part in their child's learning and experience can include open days or afternoons, newsletters, story time with siblings and show and tell events.

Multi-agency working – leading and managing in a broader team

Integrated services, mixed staffing models and the locating of early years provision within broader children's centres are increasingly more common in early childhood work. Multi-agency working brings together practitioners from different sectors and professions and is a general term used to describe a way of integrating services and support to ensure that groups – in the case of early years settings, the child – receive the most effective and useful care.

A multi-agency team working with a specific child can differ depending on the needs; it can include anyone whose work puts them in contact with the child and/or family and can therefore mean an early years manager working as part of a team with social workers, health professionals, and education. One of the key aims of multi-agency working is to provide appropriate and specific support for a child and family. This can only be achieved if the team itself can work together effectively. Once again the managing and sustaining of dialogue, clear communication and professional relationships are all essential if the team are able to work efficiently together. This is not an easy task and all involved bring their own priorities and responsibilities. For early years managers this is another aspect of their role that demands time, energy, understanding and teamwork skills.

Case study

The reality of multi-agency working

The UK's Department of Education website offers a range of case studies that can provide insights and tips for multi-agency working and the setting up of Sutton Hill children's centre, with its different stages and issues for the Sure Start team there, is one such example (www.education.gov.uk/childrenandyoungpeople/strategy/integrate dworking/a0069013/multi-agency-working, accessed 15 May 2013).

89

The wider community

At Sutton Hill, Jane Clark is the Sure Start manager. The case study sets the scene as the development of a new children's centre in one of the most deprived wards of the country, serving a local population of around 3000, 700 of whom are under five years old. Addressing and incorporating the vision and goals of Telford and Wrekin unitary authority, Jane Clark, as Sure Start programme manager, has overseen the physical building and design of the centre, as well as developed staff and services. The range of services offered include: childcare, early years learning, speech and language therapy, lifelong learning, health care support and advice, family support and play facilities. In building a staff team to support these services, there are two coordinators and a team of outreach workers who support local families. Staff are seconded from partner agencies and recruited directly and include a former teacher, a social worker, nurse, nursery nurse and a family support worker. One of the key issues for the children's centre development has been held to ensure all services are delivered in an integrated way, 'so that anyone working with a child or their family is aware of other work that is going on within the centre, and things are not duplicated or missed.'

In documenting the development of their children's centre, Jane Clark identifies three key ingredients vital for successful multi-agency working:

- a clear, targeted vision;
- excellent team building;
- shared problem solving.

So far, so good, and this echoes key themes of our discussion throughout the book so far. What has to be acknowledged, however, is that a number of practical issues can impact severely on this and so clear communication, agreed working terms, careful attention, review and creative solutions often have to be found. Let's consider how Jane and her team at Sutton Hill addressed one of the key issues of different part time staff from different agencies, working different days of the week:

- By being clear about the need for the core team to spend some time each week together, which has meant agreeing with all partner agencies that Wednesday will be one of the days that any seconded staff will work at the centre.

- By having a month's lead-in time at the centre, both to get services and equipment ready and to help people develop as a team. This induction period will provide an opportunity for team building and help all staff develop an understanding of different working cultures and structures.

- By providing training for the core team in action planning so that everyone is using the same format and working from the same starting point.

- By having regular staff meetings, both within the children's centre and as part of the broader Jubilee Sure Start programme.

- By having a shared staff room for all staff and providers to help build informal links.

(www.education.gov.uk/childrenandyoung
people/strategy/integratedworking/
a0069013/multi-agency-working)

While the premise of multi-agency working suggests a more focused, targeted and joined up approach for ensuring effective and successful care and support, the combining of different services in a team of different professionals is harder to achieve. Coordinating and managing conflicting agendas, priorities and budgets are two key reasons that make this a challenge for any early years manager. Yet multi-agency working is still recognized, along with effective leadership, as fundamental to the success of early years programmes such as Sure Start (Atkinson et al. 2001; 2002).

What does this ask of early years managers? Not only are we once again reminded of the extensive list of leadership and management skills previously discussed; the complexity, diversity and scale of early years provision in this also demands community leadership (Muijs et al. 2004; Waniganayake cited in Nivala and Hujala 2002). Community leadership expands a manager's role and remit to include the wellbeing, development and improvement of their community as well as their setting. As well as being someone to represent the community, the manager can make an important contribution as a point of liaison between the community and authorities.

The wider community just outside your door

Beyond the more obvious aspects of a wider community there are other ways the wider community can support early years managers and their settings. Fundamental to a setting surviving is keeping places filled with children; this means the wider community needs to know a setting is there and offering good care for their children. Successful marketing and advertising through the local press, with information made available at libraries, toy libraries and doctor surgeries all help to maintain a profile and presence within the community.

There are other, perhaps less obvious, ways a setting can locate and establish themselves as part of their wider community, as well as recognizing their responsibility for being part of it and being a community resource. One example of this is where a setting might find themselves in close proximity to a nursing home. To counteract inevitable complaints about noise and balls straying into their grounds, how about developing links to enable someone coming into the setting or joint carol singing.

The environmental angle is another example of how a setting forms part of a wider community resource. This could be through using the local community environment for extended and additional learning opportunities for children; or where possible, locally sourcing materials, food and drink for the setting.

Summary

There are a range of different external links and opportunities that are essential and integral to providing a good environment for staff and children and a setting as a whole. We have highlighted some obvious and perhaps less obvious relationships that an effective manager needs to be mindful of and nurture. When considering their wider community undeniably managers should prioritise parents and families as well as those overseeing the setting (governors, trustees, a board) and those parties who contribute to multi-agency working. Less blatant, but nevertheless still valuable, are the connections with the local community through the environment and other organizations and groups.

Some practical ideas for managers

A checklist

To reflect on your own good practice and links with the wider community, consider the following checklist:

1 How do those overseeing my setting know my vision and how I intend to get there?

2 How do parents and families know what my vision is for our setting?

3 How do I share my vision for the organization with other groups and the local community outside of my immediate setting?

4 What practical things do I as a manager do to establish, build and sustain positive, professional relationships with

a parents, carers and families;

b multi-agency groups;

c other community groups and people.

The wider community

5   What practical ways does your setting participate with the local community?

6   How does your setting use the local community and environment to support your children's experience and learning?

7   How does your setting source materials and supplies from the local community?

Mapping your local community

This is a practical, useful exercise to explore and map out the different, external relationships that support you as a manager and your setting. It can help with developing a plan to prioritise ways for developing your setting and working towards your vision.

1   Taking a large piece of paper mark yourself and your setting in the middle.

2   Plot on the paper all the people you liaise with, marking them nearer the middle if you liaise a lot and further out to the edge of the paper if you liaise with them less frequently.

3   Evaluate and give a mark between 1 and 10 for the quality of that relationship, where 1 = really good and 10 = not good at all.

4   Analyse your map:

   a   Who is closest to you? Do any of those closest to you have a score of 7–10? Why is this? How could you improve this relationship?

   b   What about those you have placed further away? Do they have scores of 1 or 10? What does this tell you about these relationships? Do they need to be brought closer (i.e. do you need to liaise with them more frequently)?

A similar asset and relationship mapping exercise can be done using concentric circles or with a traffic light evaluation. These tasks can also be performed as a staff team exercise to generate discussion and ideas for developing relationships further as an organization.

References

Atkinson, M., Wilkin, A., Stott, A. and Kinder, K. (2001) *Multi-Agency Working: an Audit of Activity (LGA Research Report 17)*. Slough: National Foundation for Educational Research.

Atkinson, M., Wilkin, A., Stott, A., Doherty, P. and Kinder, K. (2002) *Multi-Agency Working: a Detailed Study (LGA Research Report 26)*. Slough: National Foundation for Educational Research.

Case study: Setting up Sutton Hill children's centre, Telford & Wrekin, www.education.gov.uk/childrenandyoungpeople/strategy/integratedworking/a0069013/multi-agency-working, accessed 15 May 2013.

Muijs, D., Aubrey, C., Harris, A., and Briggs, M. (2004) How do they manage? A review of the research on leadership in early childhood, *Journal of Early Childhood Research*, 2(2), 157–60.

Nivala, V. and Hujala, E. (2002) (eds) *Leadership in Early Childhood Education, Cross Cultural Perspectives*. Oulu, Finland: Department of Educational Sciences and Teacher Education, University of Oulu.

CHAPTER 8

You as a manager and leader

Early Years leaders recognize that they do need help and support.

(Aubrey 2011: 144)

Managers have responsibility for developing themselves and others.

(Mumford 1993: xi)

To be able to deliver on a broad range of roles and responsibilities, an effective and good manager of an early years setting has a responsibility to themselves as well as the organization and everyone else within it. While many early years managers find their work immensely rewarding (Simms 2006) the demands of caring for staff, families and children, as well as the myriad of other duties, is inevitably draining and can have a detrimental impact on a manager physically, psychologically and emotionally.

Managers have a personal and professional responsibility to themselves. In addition to this, looking after themselves is integral to their responsibility of their staff team and setting. If a manager is too exhausted, stressed or simply drained to be able to do their job, then this means they cannot do their job effectively and it does not, in the long- or short-term, mean their setting has a good manager to lead them. The manager is also an important role model for other staff and what they spend time and energy on, as well as how they prioritize, will be noticed by staff.

In this chapter we will be exploring the different ways a manager can be attentive to their own well being and maintain and nourish their professional practice as an effective manager. There are several key elements for managers that should be embedded as part of their professional practice, regardless of whether they are working with their staff team, other agency partners, or the wider community. The common threads of good practice that we recommend to ensure effectiveness as a good manager and can help managers look after themselves are:

1   Consistency – in approach and expectations.
2   Clarity of communication – which includes clearly communicating your expectations and vision.
3   Clear professional relationships and boundaries.
4   Dedicated time for training and personal professional development.

Consistency

It can be challenging to retain consistency of approach across the range of different relationships and groups that a manager will come into contact with through their role. This does not mean treating them exactly the same, but it does highlight the need to have a consistent approach and expectations.

Clarity of communication

Clarity of communication is essential for managers. Not only does this help others understand a manager's expectations and priorities for the setting, but it helps the manager clearly understand this for themselves. There are two parts to clarity of communication that can be useful for managers to separate and reflect on; first there is knowing the message that needs to be delivered. An example of this is introducing new systems or meeting with parents to address a specific issue. Knowing *what* needs to be said and what outcome is wanted can help a manager more coherently and concisely express themselves and what they want.

The second part of clear communication is *how* a message is delivered. Managers may need to develop awareness of their own nonverbal communication (body language) or practise talking clearly and in a straightforward way; they may need to practise delivering messages in a group situation or handling difficult conversations and how to be assertive rather than aggressive or passive. As an insightful and extremely practical manager commented during an interview with us,

> You can have all of the glossy qualifications but if you are not able to practically communicate then you can't do much.
>
> (Interview with early years manager, May 2013)

Clear professional relationships and boundaries

Establishing clear professional relationships and boundaries help not only those around a manager, but they also support the manager in providing a framework for ensuring consistency (see above) and guidance on conduct. Where managers understand and are clear on their parameters for professional relationships this can lessen the stress and drain of managing difficult or challenging situations, or even prevent them escalating, because the manager is more aware of what to do or say.

Dedicated time for training and personal professional development

As the early years manager's role encompasses a range of leadership areas then it is understandable that any manager will require some kind of training and support to help them. Kagan and Hallmark (2001), also emphasising the need for training and development, show the need for different types of leaders in early years and single out five styles of leadership:

- Community leadership – connects childhood education to the community through informing and developing links between families, services, resources and public and private sectors.

- Pedagogical leadership – linking research and practice by disseminating new information.

- Administrative leadership – including financial and personal management.

- Advocacy leadership – contributing to long term vision of future of early years education, which also involves developing a deeper understanding of the field, legislation and being a skilled communicator.

- Conceptual leadership – conceptualizes early years leadership within the broader framework of social agendas and change.

With limited budgets and time constraints it can be extremely difficult for managers to set time and money aside for their own training and development. We have highlighted the distinct lack of adequate training and support for those who find themselves managing and leading early years teams. Once in the role of manager, the need for support and training continues; alongside changes in legislation and developments in practice, circumstances such as staffing or premises inevitably will arise that require specific and relevant training and advice.

One way managers can help themselves, and their setting, is to take practical steps to be prepared by identifying where they can go for help and advice, should they need it. Clearly it is not possible to pre-empt and second-guess every eventuality; however, identifying possible sources of support can alleviate stress and save time. Possible avenues could include: contacts within the local authority, other managers or online resources. When the need for help and support then arises they have options in place for making informed decisions and resolving the situation swiftly and professionally.

Bringing these threads together within the staff team

In any staff team there are certainly going to be individuals who are easier to get on with than others. Good managers treat staff equally (no favourites) and can clearly communicate what they want from their staff. When it is necessary managers are also able to use assertiveness to deal with and resolve challenges and difficult situations. This may be related to staff performance, relationships within the team or introducing change to a setting. Through this consistency and clear communication good managers recognize they may not, on occasions, be liked for their decisions or demands, but they also will earn greater respect from their team and be confident that their staff team understand what is being asked of them.

Managers communicate their expectations informally and formally with their team. Both are important. More formal individual conversations, as well as staff training, staff meetings and regular supervision are opportunities to maintain dialogue with staff and for managers to know that they are supporting their team. In desire to offer emotional as well as professional support for staff there is a note of caution to be made here – managers should be careful that sessions do not slip into counselling; emotional support is often needed but this should not and cannot go beyond professional boundaries. These boundaries may need to be explicitly set out by the manager with their team. Again, this helps the team and the manager in understanding their roles and responsibilities.

It is paramount that managers are able to establish and maintain professional relationships with colleagues, as well as other groups such as parents and other agencies. This can be particularly difficult in small communities where the boundaries between managers and staff and parents can get blurred. Nevertheless the manager has a key role in modelling and upholding professional boundaries and professional dialogue. This sets the tone and norms for how others act and talk. This also supports the manager as lapsing into a situation where colleagues, or parents, become your 'mate' can leave a manager exposed and vulnerable, especially when circumstances may call for the manager to challenge or bring a difficult situation up for discussion.

Delegation and distributing roles is another way a manager supports themselves and their setting. Initially this may require an investment of time and support from the manager. For example, a staff member may need to shadow a manager, work alongside them, or simply have a series of one-to-one meetings, before taking on new responsibilities. Delegating duties without providing clear parameters, adequate instruction and support does not usually save time as neither the manager or member of staff will have sufficient confidence or understanding of the task. In the longer term this does not support the organization – or the manager who simply makes more work for themselves if they are required to spend time and energy resolving problems later.

There are different ways that managers can support and train staff to share duties and responsibilities. This helps the managers and also contributes to skilling up future early years managers. Depending on the tasks being delegated managers can help themselves and develop other managers through training, instruction, tutoring, personal coaching and personal counselling (Mumford 1993: 203). Not all of this has to be done by sending staff out to external courses; much of it can be achieved through onsite support and shadowing.

Bringing these threads together through the wider community

Managers can gain a deeper understanding and confidence in their role in different ways. They can learn from their experiences intuitively (instinctively), incidentally (through a chance occurrence), retrospectively (by looking back at a past event or situation) and prospectively (something that may happen in the future) (Mumford 1993: 19). Whereas some of this will take place within the early years setting itself, managers can gain broader insights and understanding by stepping back and out of the immediate situation.

The wider community offers ways that managers can help themselves in their role with this. Focused and personal one-to-one supervision can be greatly beneficial, as can links with networks and training with others managers in the area. In addition to training, offering new and up-to-date information provides time for reflection, an opportunity to gain perspective and consider their organization as a whole.

On a day-to-day basis many managers will find that the pressures and demands on them and pace of work do not allow space to think or reflect more broadly. Not only is time away with other managers or for further training important as a point for reflection. More generally, managers need to give themselves permission to switch off and stop. Ensuring a work/life balance is not just an entitlement, it ensures wellbeing and stamina physically and emotionally so that managers can do their job effectively. It also sets an important example to other staff about valuing and taking responsibility for oneself. Early years managers will always have further paperwork, issues to deal with and matters to follow up and sort out. Being able to stop, switch off and walk away can be difficult. It can also provide valuable time for processing and returning to work and the role with fresh eyes and renewed energy.

References

Aubrey, C. (2011) *Leading and Managing in the Early Years*. London: Sage.

Kagan, S. L. and Hallmark, L. G. (2001) Cultivating leadership in early care and education, *Child Care Information Exchange*, 140: 7–10.

Mumford, A. (1993) *How Managers Can Develop Managers*. London: Gower.

Simms, M. (2006) 'Retention of early years and childcare practitioners in private day nurseries: is love enough?' Paper presented at the British Educational Research Association New Researchers/Student Conference, University of Warwick, 6 September 2006.

CHAPTER 9

Conclusion

We want to draw this book to a close with a final overview on how to use the material and a reminder of its intended audience, the current climate in early years and a look into the future for managers and leaders. When we were writing this book we were thinking that it would be of interest and use to those practitioners who are already leaders and managers of settings. We were also thinking of those early years workers who were aspiring to be managers and leaders. We have long considered that managing and leading teams should be an integral part of the basic and the enhanced training of practitioners and wanted this book to be accessible to those who were in the earlier stages of training as well as people completing foundation degrees and EYPS programmes.

The one sure thing that can be said about an early years setting is that there is no standard model. There is probably no other workforce sector that has such a varied and diverse range of settings and also profiles of people working in those settings. The truth is that it is mainly women who work in early years. Having said that there is a small but growing number of men who are choosing work with under fives and are a welcome addition to the workforce. This work with babies and children attracts to its workforce people at all points on the age spectrum, a fusion of nationalities and to some extent also a mix of social classes of people. One of the reasons for this is that many women come into childcare after having children of their own and being attracted to the thought of working with other people's children, using the skills they have acquired with their own families. In the case of childminders they can do that while also remaining at home caring for their own under fives.

When thinking about classifying the types of settings that there are in the early years sector we can think about nurseries, child-minders, crèches, and pre-schools. Within those wide and loose classifications there are subdivisions of children's centres, private nurseries that are individual, those that are part of a chain, workplace nurseries, nurseries that are part of schools, crèches that support conferences and projects, those that are in health clubs, pre-schools that were set up and are still run by local parents, groups of childminders who operate as a small nursery – the list is exhaustive. This classification does not take into account the further diversity that is around the catchment area of the nursery, whether it is urban or rural, which part of the country it is in, if it is attached to a school and the culture and ethos of the school – again, the list is endless.

Within that large diverse group there is a unifying factor. Everyone has as their paramount focus the well being of children at the core of their practice. We suggest in the book that this simple focus can be a very powerful uniting force when thinking about inspiring leading. This leading can be in the face of resistance from staff teams or individuals and also against the backdrop of a workforce who have to constantly manage change and increased expectations from parents and public bodies while struggling with low wages and often difficult working conditions.

The future

As we are writing this book (May 2013) there is a mixed outlook to the future of early years in terms of managing and leading. The recent Government publication 'More Great Childcare' advocates increased staff–child ratios and the withdrawal of support from local authorities. It relies heavily on the French model of childcare provision and has been opposed by many early years bodies, for example the National Children's Bureau. However, these possible changes are still being debated and there is a mood of cautious optimism in many quarters that there may not have to be backward steps and some settings will choose to remain at the current ratios even if the proposed changes do come in. (www.nurseryworld.co.uk, accessed 20 May 13.)

Taking the long view, the standard and quality of early years provision has improved in the UK over the last twenty years and many of these changes are part of a clock that cannot be turned back. There is an expectation from parents and carers that early years workers are well trained, regularly inspected and work to a curriculum that is play based. A programme of work-based training and qualifications means that leaders and managers of settings are and will continue to be better equipped to deal with the increased demands of the job than they were in the past.

The managers of the future

Trying to have a crystal ball view of the future of managing and leading is very hard. We have established that the main certainty is uncertainty and change and this shows no sign of abating. The manager of the future will have to be someone who sees the challenge but also the opportunities in change and is able to accommodate it into current practice. Along with the rest of the workforce a manager will have to be flexible and continually able to update and enhance their practice in line with the changing expectations of Government initiative, statutory bodies and parents and carers. As with any business the owners have to respond to market demands and so settings need to look at elements such as opening hours and days, the quality of the food they serve, and the facilities that are offered in order to provide a service that meets the expectations of parents/carers.

Conclusion

Staff turnover

The most important underpinning element guiding practice should be the needs of the children and one of the keystones of providing a secure environment for children is having a stable staff team. With this stable team the children are able to build close and trusting relationships with their keyworkers. This is the rock on which the children's growth and development flourishes. With this underpinning security children can feel empowered to explore and make sense of the world around them and engage in sustained shared thinking with staff who are an integral part of their world away from the home environment. Having a stable staff team affects every aspect of the settings work and has wide-ranging consequences. It also provides security for the parents and carers who use the setting. With the relationships that they are able to build with practitioners they are better equipped to trust the care and education that is offered by the setting and less likely to worry about their children while they are at the setting. A purely economic view of this would say that the parents' ability to engage in work and contribute to the country's economy is enhanced by having childcare arrangements that are stable and give the worker confidence, allowing them to return to work after having children and also to focus on their work fully. This, of course, is assuming that returning to work is the ideal state for parents and this is a keystone debate among thinkers and writers in early years.

In terms of safeguarding children, having a stable staff team can mean that children are more likely to trust and disclose to their keyworker and parents and carers are also more likely to seek help and advice or disclose abuse to the staff at the early years setting. If the child has a close relationship over a period of time with a keyworker then that worker is able to foster resilience in that child – to provide them with emotional 'credit' for times that might be difficult.

> While individual attributes may be important it should be remembered that resilience emerges in a supportive context.
>
> (Gilligan 2009: 6)

A stable staff team are also more likely to observe a child who has additional needs and be able to work long-term with the child and parents/carers to support and meet the needs of all concerned. Also, taking this idea into a wider context, having a stable staff team in a well-established early years setting means that the setting is more likely to be part of the wider community and establish links with local people and services.

With this in mind the manager of the future needs to be able to recruit and also retain a motivated and focused staff team. We have given some pointers as to the most effective way to do this. The manager/owner will also have to think carefully about staff conditions and wages in order to attract the highest calibre of staff and retain them. This alone will help the setting in terms of the service it offers, the families that it attracts to use the setting, and the profile that it has locally and in terms of inspection. When funds are low, investment in staff is always a good use of resources, and the manager of the future will need to see this.

Paper trails

When working with early years teams we often hear discussion that managing a setting is now over-reliant on paper evidence of children's progress and the settings adherence to legislative standards. Managers worry that fulfilling these demands is taking practitioners and managers away from the job of face-to-face contact with children. When we have asked managers what are the main difficulties of the job the reply came back without hesitation:

> Paperwork and managing change. There is not enough thought put into the changes. Lots of time it is the same stuff but just expressed in a different way. You put a programme into place

Conclusion

and then something new comes in and you have to update it. This adds to the stress of the job and makes you doubt your good practice just because it is looks different from the current thinking.

(Early years manager)

We acknowledge that organizing such procedures has its difficulties, but we also believe that designing, planning, adapting and implementing how the recording practice can enhance the safety and development of the children in their care can unify not only the staff and management team but also the setting and the parents/carers. Reviewing and updating such systems is a loadstone of practice that can be used to bond settings teams and the communities in which they are placed in times of struggle and difficulty. It is important when introducing change to a setting that the manager picks out how this change will improve practice and how to adapt changes in order to fit in with current good practice. Of course it might also be that current practice needs to be changed in order to meet altered expectations and demands and this should always be seen as a possibility. Fullan (1993: 14) writes about the 'mastery' of change – how teachers (and I have extended this to early years) have to be skilled in new ideas, to really understand how they fit rather than just know them. It is this practical way of looking at elements of change and then putting theory into practice that the early years manager of the future needs to become adept at in order to make their setting relevant and current.

Finally

This emphasis on the well being of the children that forms the driving force for every development in early years practice has ultimately also been our focus during the writing of this book. We believe that a well-managed and led staff team who are inspired by a skilled and creative head of a setting can only add to and enhance the development and well being of the children they care for. If we have been talking mainly about the relationships and interactions between adults in this book it is only to support and underpin the work that they are doing with children.

The prime concern of any setting, any manager, any practitioner, should be the care and development of the children that they interact with and in order to make this practice reach the highest standards a motivated team works with an inspirational leader in order to nurture and grow the adults of tomorrow.

The final words in this book should go to a pre-school manager. We asked her what advice she would give to herself twenty years ago when she was just starting as a manager of a committee-run 'pack away' pre-school based in a church hall. Her reply was:

> I would say keep on going. Looking back I would say that I have always been a good leader, manager and team player as well but I didn't always trust my own skills. I would say to believe in my own instincts, go with the gut feeling, keep steady and true. Be respectful and keep working hard in order to set a good example to my team.

References

Fullan, M. G. (1993) Why teachers must become change agents, *Educational Leadership.* 50(6): March.

Gilligan, R. (2009) *Promoting resilience: Supporting children and young people who are in care, adopted or in need.* London: British Association for Adoption & Fostering.

Index

Italics refer to entries in tables.

Index

Index